DOYLER

MICK DOYLE

GILL AND MACMILLAN

Published in Ireland
by Gill and Macmillan Ltd
Goldenbridge
Dublin 8
with associated companies in
Auckland, Budapest, Gaborone, Harare, Hong Kong,
Kampala, Kuala Lumpur, Lagos, London, Madras,
Manzini, Melbourne, Mexico City, Nairobi,
New York, Singapore, Sydney, Tokyo, Windhoek
© Mick Doyle 1991
First published in hardback 1991
This paperback edition published 1992
0 7171 2026 0
Print origination by
Seton Music Graphics Ltd, Bantry, Co. Cork
Printed by Colour Books Ltd, Dublin

A catalogue record is available for this book
from the British Library

I dedicate this autobiography — *Doyler* — primarily to Mandy and Lynne, my children Andrew, Sharon, Amanda and Emma, to our families past and present, and of course to all those people with whom I have been involved, and to whom I am indebted during my first 50 years on this earth.

September 1991

Contents

List of Illustrations

Foreword

This book, naturally, is a very personal story; it has as its catalyst the RTE 'Gay Byrne Show' on a Friday morning in February 1987, the day before Ireland beat England.

Gay, in his inimitable, forthright, but highly sensitive, probing manner, helped me to articulate publicly the very private traumas and tribulations of our marriage breakdown and how Lynne and myself came to terms with it.

Possibly the fact that I was a supposedly macho, high-profile coach to the Irish rugby team lent a somewhat different slant to my experiences — however, the public's awareness and response to that interview was quite extraordinary and to this day people approach me to talk of how they related to its frankness and content and the help it has apparently been to many of them. Naturally, I am both touched and honoured.

Obviously, human life is a great teacher provided we have the proper classroom and are willing to learn.

Self-editing is a taxing discipline; with much help I forced myself to leave out so many incidents of interest.

Because of its nature and abbreviated length, this story is akin to a leisurely journey through the varied terrain of my life, offering changing views of some important scenarios from the corridors and galleries of my mind. It pauses now and then at various signposts for more close-up views of my life's landscapes and milestones.

I wrote my story partly in the belief that it may offer some insights into 'life in the fast lane' and its destructive fellow travellers, and in the hope that it may suggest some answers to someone less fortunate than me who may find themselves in a temporary 'limbo'.

Mostly, however, I wrote it for the fun and vanity of having my life's story published and for the opportunity it offered to bring some people and events central to my life into proper focus.

Writing this manuscript has generated powerful emotions within me — of sadness, loneliness, loss of those departed, nostalgia and wistfulness, but most of all of joy, happiness, achievement and a profound sense of gratitude towards so many people.

It is an honest book, at least an honest attempt at an autobiography. I hope you enjoy reading it.

I owe much to Lynne for the honourable way in which we addressed out marriage failure. My relationship with Mandy provided me with the love, perspective and confidence to write openly, without fear about my life.

It is they, my children and all my friends in my sport who, in the final analysis, contributed to my development as a person and gave me anything worth a damn to write about.

And of course, were it not for Gay Byrne's classroom you might never have known.

Mick Doyle

Acknowledgments

In January 1989, P.J. Cunningham, *Evening Herald*, at the suggestion of Brian Jaffray, then a freelance journalist with that paper, flattered me into beginning a series of bi-weekly 'scribblings' for the *Evening Herald* on my 'second' favourite topic — rugby.

As the gamble apparently paid off P.J. further inveigled me to write my life story and Fergal Tobin, editor with Gill and Macmillan, to publish it. P.J.'s lovely wife, Rosemary, took on the onerous task of deciphering my hand-written manuscript and typed it into recognisable form.

Fergal and P.J. further helped me to refine the script and edit it down to an acceptable length.

My wife Mandy ensured that the text fell within the bounds of 'normality'.

I am indebted for their enlightened opinions and wish to acknowledge sincerely their invaluable contributions.

I also wish to thank my youngest daughter Emma (2) for adjusting her sleeping habits to accommodate my early morning writings and my canine family members — Rambles, Grouse (since deceased), Buffy, Bunty and Beanie for their understanding and patience.

1

An Affair of the Heart

'All rumours of my death are grossly exaggerated.'
(MARK TWAIN, ALIAS SAMUEL LONGHORNE CLEMENS, MID 1800s)

A GENTLE hand vibrated my body. I tried valiantly not to wake up but failed. My mind was responding in slow motion, running relentlessly through the familiar check list: testicles, spectacles, vallet and vatch!

Someone deep inside my head was silently screaming 'Where in the name of Jaysus am I?' My tactile senses told me that I was wearing a smock, and sporting a dog-tag on my left wrist instead of my watch. I was cocooned in a narrow bed and at least all my procreating/leisure equipment was present. I assumed that I was still Michael G. Doyle, veterinarian, businessman, father, lover, ex-husband, friend and coach to the Irish Rugby Football team.

The Irish rugby team! The World Cup, Auckland, New Zealand, May 1987. Again I thought — where am I and what am I doing wherever I am? Where are all the lads? As the almost imperceptible attempts to wake me continued quietly I did some visual reconnoitring. The bed was in a cubicle: lots of equipment stared at me and graphs zig-zagged all over the place like the mayfly on the Corrib.

Faintly I could make out other cubicles, beds and formless faces in the muted light of what could only be a hospital ward.

The vibrator's persistence was finally rewarded and the lovely face and form of a young New Zealand nurse materialised

1

before my eyes. She whispered softly 'Michael, Michael, are you awake?'

'How could I stay asleep with all the racket you created' I answered. 'Where am I anyway?'

'You're in the Coronary Care Unit of Auckland General Hospital. You've had a coronary incident and are under observation here, and you are to relax.'

'By the way,' says she, 'there's someone for you on the phone from Ireland called Haughey. Do you want to talk to him ?'

As she went off to the nurses' station to connect up my phone I could hear peals of girlish laughter emanating from a group of excited nurses — obviously delighted to be talking to Charles J. Haughey, Prime Minister of Ireland as if he were a long lost friend. He was most certainly charming them. Next thing he was charming me.

'Doyler,' says the Taoiseach, 'What are you doing there? Uncle Gaybo (Gay Byrne) was telling the nation on the radio here at home this morning of your sudden hospitalisation and we all wish you the best of luck and a speedy recovery.'

Before I could trade witticisms with him he cracked 'I bet you're only just suffering Guinness withdrawal pangs.'

I replied that I was merely taking a career break. He inquired about the medical service, care and attention. I said they were superb.

He asked if it was as good as at home. I was tempted to reply that at least it hadn't been closed in the last 24 hours, but I desisted. I am noted for my decorum, you see.

We traded good wishes for a while and then he was gone with the words 'Look after yourself Doyler, you're very important to all of us.'

I shall never forget Charlie Haughey's phone call that day. As long as I live I will maintain a vivid recollection of it; mainly because he bothered to phone with warm and kind words to me when I needed them most. A true reflection of the man.

I was left with no doubt that, on that particular morning in May 1987, lying in the Coronary Care Unit in Auckland, I was the most important Irishman in the whole world.

I told this to Syd Millar who visited me with Dr Mick Molloy shortly afterwards and he replied: 'Bollox, Doyler, shure you're only a jumped-up Kerryman!'

Syd was our team manager and Mick our doctor — both good mates from way back — and both looked after my well-being in incredible fashion during the world cup campaign in New Zealand and Australia.

Later that afternoon Derek McKeen and Harry Rea visited me as did Ewart Bell and his wife and Brian Wain and his better half.

Derek McKeen is from Dungannon but had become head of Auckland's metropolitan motorised police planning section. Dr Harry Rea had settled in New Zealand in the early seventies — I had played with him for Ireland in 1967–68.

Sir Ewart Bell, President of the IRFU, was in New Zealand as guest of the World Rugby Cup Committee.

Ewart had been an Irish selector during my playing career and I had always found him a courteous, honourable man and a good friend.

Brian Wain is an ould UCD/Garryowen rugby-playing friend from Cork; if Wainey got you at the tail-end of a loose ruck, he had a way about him, like Munster forwards of yore, of persuading you not to lie on the ball. He was in New Zealand for the rugby, to see relatives, and for the craic. I was truly delighted to see them all — I was even more delighted to be alive.

As that Monday afternoon progressed into the kind of peaceful, reflective timelessness especially peculiar to hospitals and encircled as I was by caring staff and other patients , it was easy to retrace languidly the sequence of events which had brought me to this oasis of medical care in the first place.

Having arrived in Auckland completely and utterly exhausted at the end of a 36-hour journey from London (Gatwick) on Saturday we had checked into our hotel.

Later in the afternoon we did some light training at a local Marist ground and had an early night.

Syd Millar, our team manager, had organised a scrummaging session with the Scottish forwards for Sunday morning and I took our prima donnas (the backs) out for a session on that beautiful morning.

Being overweight by about three stones (20 kgs), out of condition and highly stressed, I was in no fit state to indulge in the usual jogging, limbering-up exercises, push-ups and sit-ups that my players were doing as routine. But then I knew of no team which had ever won because their coach was fit!

Even Hugo MacNeill, normally the Grand Wizard of piss-takers, had advised me to slow down with the well-chosen words, 'Stop showing off Doyler, will you.'

This of course drove me to higher paroxysms of aerobic endeavour and I just managed to crawl in for a shower by lunch-time.

During the afternoon Syd and Mannix (Donal Lenihan, our captain), came to my room to select the team for our first match against Wales in Wellington.

We got ready to leave the hotel by about 5.30 p.m. to attend the opening ceremonies at another location.

Downstairs, as we assembled in the lobby with other teams the atmosphere was carnival-like.

The Western Samoans were striking, nay startling, in their grey dress blazers with skirts instead of trousers. I couldn't help but picture half a dozen of these huge virile bulls of men being let loose for a weekend at Lisdoonvarna!

So I was sitting on a table day-dreaming about Samoan stallions in the County Clare and chatting to Philip Orr and Mick Molloy when suddenly the room was spinning around me — slowly mark you, but spinning nevertheless.

With Dr Molloy's assent, I decided to go to bed, have a light dinner and knock myself out with two sleeping tablets and hopefully sleep until 9 a.m. on Monday.

Luxuriating on the bed and ready to order a mouth-watering seafood dinner, I reached for the phone and wham — it hit me!

The most singularly searing pain I had ever experienced lasted some seconds and was followed by a slow, methodical squeezing in my chest — on the left-hand side — that seemed to go on for hours.

It felt like a strong hand had entered my chest cavity, grabbed my heart and was proceeding to flatten it against my rib-cage.

Immediately I thought 'Dear Jesus, I'm having a heart attack.' Fear struck next and I found myself hyperventilating. I stopped myself from breathing too quickly and began a slow deep-breathing routine.

I phoned the front desk and told the operator my problem and to please call Dr Mick Molloy at the 'atrocities' at the other side of the city. They knew where he was.

Things became funnier after that. The hotel doctor was out in his boat, but would be with me as soon as possible. Meanwhile the assistant manager and the accountant arrived at my door without any keys. I had to get out of bed and walk through two rooms to let them in. Talk about having a heart attack in peace: coronary incident me arse!

I was in severe pain and doubled up. Since none of us knew whether I should keep my head above my limbs or my legs above my head, I tried to do both — like a bloody contortionist!

I shaped myself into a V and achieved the impossible.

The two hotel men, gentlemen to the core, kept me talking about home and rugby and succeeded in keeping my mind off the pain while allowing me to concentrate on whatever one does to handle a heart attack when you're a few million miles away from home on your own in a hotel room, while your mates are guzzling on caviar and champagne a few miles away . . . forty-six years old and riding off into the sunset!

I almost wished I'd let Willie John McBride keep the bloody coaching job in the first place. Almost, but not quite.

The house doctor and Mick Molloy arrived almost simultaneously (and 'at the same time as well' as Mick Cuddy might say) with the ambulance men and paramedics. Between them they sorted me out, calmed me down and marvelled at how cool I was. Cool — I was scared shitless! I earned at least an Oscarette.

Anyway, they got me to the hospital where I underwent some preliminary checks by a quite strikingly efficient and friendly cardiac team before arriving in bed in the coronary care ward and being connected up to the medical paraphernalia.

Later my darling wife Mandy phoned me and I experienced her love, devotion and prayer at all that distance.

Believe me I could feel and appreciate the power of healing love in my body from the moment she spoke of it to me and it took away all the pent-up, inexplicable fear and distrust of the unexpected.

Lynne, my former wife, for whom I have enormous respect and affection, also phoned with love and best wishes from our children Andrew, Sharon, Amanda and friends.

After that the next thing I remember was Charlie Haughey ringing me up out of the blue.

2

In the Beginning

IN the chilly pre-dawn hours of October 13 1940, a corpulent paracodeine-sodden Reichsmarschall, Herman Goering (Hoyman de Goiman) rattled off a telegram to his awaiting Luftwaffe bigwigs, which read something like this: 'Ziss iss Operation Eagle ! Vizin ze shorrt periott you vill vipe out ze Britisher Air Force from der sky at night. Heil Hitler ! Und up affzer you!'

At exactly the same time, approximately, another momentous event was taking place. A pewling, weakling infant who was to become Michael Gerard Martin Doyle emerged into the world, into the idyllic Camelot of 'Riverside' Currow, Farranfore, Co. Kerry. Newly-born to Nell and Michael Doyle, the infant Doyler was to spend the early months of his life in the simulated womb of an oxygen tent until his health, weight, bodily functions and dangly bits stabilised themselves.

From these world-shattering beginnings it has been downhill ever since.

Riverside on the Brown Flesk river, was and still is the ancestral home of the Dennehy clan — descendants of Tom and Molly Dennehy. Tom originated from Meelin country,

7

in Co. Cork and Molly Hayes from the Cork/Limerick border near Broadford, not too far from the Sullivans of Tournafulla. They begat seven children, Bill, Paddy, Humphrey, Tom and Sean and two girls Ellen (Nell) and Mai. Sadly only Sean remains and lives in the charming old house with his wife Eileen and a menagerie of springers, retrievers, setters and rabbits.

Nell Dennehy was born in Meelin, Co. Cork but spent most of her early life in Riverside, Currow.

Like most young girls she loved horses and dogs. She was also an excellent camogie player — full of skill and spirit. She was a beautiful lively girl with peach complexion and auburn hair.

She took her pony with her to the boarding school run by an order of French nuns at Drishane near Millstreet in Co. Cork. Academic pursuits were far from being a priority for young ladies in the early 1930s.

Her father Tom Dennehy had established the Dicksgrove Group of Creameries (now part of Kerry Group PLC) and could afford to educate his children in the desired manner.

Nell went to finishing school in Monaco's Convent de Saint Maur in 1933 and naturally became a fluent French speaker and a very cultured young lady, possessed of all the social graces and an eminently desirable future wife for some lucky fellow. Naturally she had lots of admirers and boyfriends as had her sister Mai. Whereas Nell was quiet and shy at first, Mai was totally extrovert. These traits became accentuated as they grew older. They were enormously fond of each other and became inseparable.

Michael J. P. Doyle's mother died when he was two years old and his father Mike brought up his four children, Thomas, Mary Agnes, Kit and Michael as well as he could. He was a relatively successful general merchant/publican in Castleisland, Co. Kerry.

Michael went as a boarder to Newbridge College, Co. Kildare early in 1930 and there he developed his enduring love of rugby and his superb in-depth knowledge of the game and all that it offers. But his father's ill-health brought a sadly premature end to his boarding school days. Young Michael had to come home to run the business.

He was a romantic young sport and fell in and out of love with painful regularity. He loved all women. He had a 'serious' girlfriend in Killorglin and used to cycle from Castleisland — a round trip of about 60 miles — to see her every weekend. She was his first great love and they walked hand in hand along the banks of the lazy river Laune stopping for the occasional cuddle. At least that's what he told me! The affair ended when she went off to Eccles Street College in Dublin.

He had a great affinity for girls (what's new?) which naturally enough prompted the age old question 'How will I know the right one when she comes along?'.

His Uncle Denny, his great friend, advised him that breeding was an all-important trait in a girl. He said: 'If you're only digging for worms to go fishing, Michael, look for worms with breeding!'

'That's all very well,' replied the young Romeo, 'but how would you recognise it in a girl?' The reply was startling in the simplicity of its logic. 'If she has it, she wants nothing else, but if she hasn't got it, nothing else will do her.'

Armed with this 'formula for life', the ardent young blade searched many a likely spot for a nubile young female with breeding. He was often disappointed.

As luck had it, a rugby-playing friend, Bill Dennehy, a Blackrock College boy, invited Michael to meet his family in Currow and, 'Bingo', Michael met his Nell. It was instant attraction on both sides and there started a love affair that endured until her untimely death. To this day he loves her with the truth and passion of a new love and I, his son, adore him for it. After a very short time they became engaged on Halloween night in 1939. They sealed their pledge to each other with a barm brack ring. Dad still has that ring. The official engagement ring was lovingly selected at Weir's in Grafton Street, Dublin, soon after.

A beautiful, sunny day dawned in Currow on 4 January 1940. They were married in the old village Church, had their wedding breakfast at Riverside and spent their wedding night at the Old Ground Hotel, Ennis, Co. Clare — Jack Donnelly wasn't there then! They spent their honeymoon in the West, in Galway and Mayo and knowing my mother, they had to spend at least two days shopping in Dublin, locating themselves at the old Jury's Hotel in Dame Street.

As Dad recalls it I made my presence felt with great rapidity and the main worry was that I wouldn't wait the obligatory nine months. To everybody's relief, I emerged on 13 October 1940 — giving them nine days peace of mind!

My mother was confined to bed for most of her pregnancy due to a serious illness and was far too weak to look after her new-born Micheál. The then unmarried Auntie Mai brought me up unselfishly and heaped on me all the devotion, attention and love that Mammy could not physically give me at the time. My brother Tom was born 4½ years after me. I lived in Currow with my grandparents and Mai, Humphrey and Sean while he lived with my parents in Castleisland. I barely knew him or my parents for quite a few years. It all seems so strange now but at the time that was the way it had to be.

I went to Ranalough National School from age 4 to 12 and was extremely lucky to come under the influence of three teachers whose dedication left an indelible impression on me — Con Geaney, Margaret Meredith and Tim Keane.

Con imbued in me an enduring love and passion for Gaelic football, having represented Kerry himself. Margaret Meredith instilled and nurtured in me a love of English literature and books in general. She made me do all the English reading in our class.

I doubt very much if any schoolboy anywhere had a more superbly gifted, intelligent and caring schoolteacher than we had in Tim Keane. Where Con and Margaret could be demons with 'the rod' Tim Keane publicly burned all canes in the school on his first day. This did not prevent you from collecting a corrective clip across the ear from his open hand but his method of teaching was to help children to understand.

At the time, in the 1940s and 50s, life in rural Ireland was harsh and luxuries like new shoes and new clothes were rare. Many of my school mates came to school cold and without shoes in winter. Many children of small farmers came to school exhausted from milking cows by hand in the early morning and from other farm chores. They had to repeat the process in the evenings when they went home. Add to this the lack of electricity in any home in rural Ireland at that time — certainly in Kerry — and you can appreciate that many children had neither time nor opportunity for homework. Tim Keane knew this and to his eternal credit and I hope, eternal reward, he found his own solution: any child who didn't know his lessons wasn't slapped but was kept back after official classes ended so that they could learn in suitable surroundings and receive the educational help their parents were incapable of providing.

For my last three years in Currow National School I stayed back each evening with about five companions for extra-curricular tuition: he took the 'brightest' kids and helped them to learn more about each subject. This group included his son Maurice who was highly intelligent. The other children kept back to learn their normal lessons revelled in such an atmosphere of calm, positive education.

There are many people today including me who owe Tim Keane an incalculable debt. He was also a fair man and an excellent conversationalist — he didn't treat you like a child and you responded accordingly.

Every single morning, no matter what the weather was doing all of us walked towards his home and met him and young Maurice as they came over the brow of the hill that led down into our sleepy village. He addressed all the boys in turn and asked of each 'Bhfuil aon scéal agatsa?' (Have you any story for me?) We even made up stories to impress him. When my brother Tom was first sent to Currow School during my last year there he ran away on the first day — a feat that was unheard of in Currow, because there was no need to: nobody was afraid. Having attended the convent school in Castleisland he had obviously learned damn all and I had to spend an hour each day teaching him how to write his name and do his 'tables'. He learned well and is now a bit of a financial genius. His writing isn't bad either!

The school prepared us for many college scholarship entrance examinations — we usually pulled off at least two annually. I know I qualified for scholarships for three secondary colleges. However, I was sent to Newbridge College in Co. Kildare and I am glad of that.

Being in Kerry of course, we were all Gaelic football mad and we loved to join in 'Backs and Forwards' with the big men — the Shanahans, the Dennehys, the Breens, the Flemings and others.

Since my grandparents had the only radio in the village for quite a long time I have vivid memories of sitting among a crowd of adults on Sunday afternoons listening to Radio Éireann and Michael O'Hehir's stirring commentaries from playing fields up and down Ireland as well as from the polo grounds in New York. The GAA should have made him president for life or a millionaire or something, because he could make a lively, stirring encounter out of the dullest, most one-sided match you ever saw. I think Michael could inject passion and commitment into tossing the coin for choice of ends!

I remember great names like Joe Keohane, Bill Casey, Paddy Bawn Brosnan (a good friend of mine), Roundy Landers, 'Gega' Connor, Paddy Kennedy, Mick Higgins, Paddy Prendergast and countless others.

I collected a lot of money, mainly from my grandfather, to buy an O'Neill's pigskin football in 1951. We had a good school team and travelled regularly on Sundays to other school parishes like Currans and Scartaglen to play their local world beaters. We travelled on foot, occasionally by bicycle but mostly by donkey and cart. We had fights with 'tinkers' coming home, robbed orchards and organised donkey derbies with various farmers' noble asses.

My grandfather taught me how to long and high jump, Uncle Humphrey ('Free') taught me a love of dogs, gardening and hand-ball and Uncle Sean taught me how to shoot from a pellet gun (airgun) and rifle and how to drive a car. My grandmother, Momma Dennehy, taught me how to learn my lessons, bake bread, lay the table and look after myself.

We made extra pocket money — my cousins Liam and Hugh Dennehy, Dan 'Jeffrey' Fleming and myself — by catching rabbits and picking blackberries.

We went live open coursing on Sundays in winter — Hugh and I had the greyhounds, or else we 'borrowed' (i.e. stole) one for the day; Dan 'Jeffrey' usually provided the terrier to drive the rabbits out from the bushes. We had to be extra nice to Dan, and he knew it because at the slightest provocation, real or imagined, the little bollox would whistle for his terrier and shag off home leaving us to pretend that we were the terriers!

I can still smell the new-mown hay — the cleanest, freshest smell in the world. I had almost forgotten it until we spent our June 1990 holidays in Kenmare. The soporific aroma of newly-cut and newly-turned hay along the Sneem road brought back the clacking sounds of the horse-drawn mowing machine, the corn crake, the sound of the train between Farranfore and Tralee, welcome intrusions on the peaceful stillness of my village in the 1940s and 50s.

We spent every summer on Uncle Bill and Auntie Mary's farm at Ballybeg and all of us cousins were falling over one another to help. I had a million cousins in Currow. Bill and Mary's family were Tom, Marie, Margaret, Hugh, the 'two' twins Helen and Catherine and Liam. Humphrey and Mary had Tom (now tragically deceased), Maureen and Joan. Young Bernie wasn't born then.

My 'second' cousins, children of Paddy and Julia Dennehy — Humphrey, Tom, Paddy, Winnie, Sheila, Peg, Anna, Breda and Norrie — were mostly older.

I was resident at Riverside — the various cousins spent some time there in relative captivity but they didn't have a look in. I was the favourite and that was the end of it, they keep reminding me. They also help me recall the naughty things I did to them while we were growing up — especially Helen and Catherine. It is a wonder they are still alive after all I was supposed to have done to them. I loved them all then as I do now — probably more now, as well as all their families.

I got to know Uncle Denny and cousins Mary and Den O'Sullivan in Castleisland during my teens, as I did the Dennehys in Dublin — Ken, Jeanette, Linda, Tom and Jean's family and Tommie and Mary Dennehy in Skibbereen, Paddy and Mary's family. If I don't mention them in my one and only autobiography they will ostracise me for life.

On my Dad's side there was Kit and Jim Wyse and their family, Jo, Anne, James, Michael, Barry and Fiona; and Tom and Madge Doyle's family in Ballyheigue — Mike, Frank and all the girls.

I remember once around 1958–9 at a dance in Tralee I spent a lot of time chatting up a gorgeous girl, successfully I might add. As she was about to get her coat at the dance's end I asked her name. She was my cousin from Ballyheigue. Full marks to her though. She went back in and came out with a lovely girl so that I wouldn't be empty-handed. Delia, wherever you are, you were good fun and great company; and cousin, you're something else too!

I learned how to fish for salmon and trout from John Rahilly, an octogenarian, Paddy Bat Shanahan and Tom Sean O'Connor from Castleisland. Tom was also the water bailiff and as good an acquirer of salmon as I have ever seen!

One day we were installed at a favourite pool on the Brown Flesk river below the creamery, fishing with worms amid a rising, raging flood, when three Tralee fishermen (we knew they were from Tralee by the gear they had) arrived, as if they had been beamed up by Scottie from Starship Enterprise, and inquired of Tom Sean, my instructor — 'Excuse me Sir, is it deep in dere?'

Now 'in dere' was evidently the deepest, most treacherous part of the bloody river.

Tom replied rapidly 'Bejaysus lads, you wouldn't have to go too far in dere before you wouldn't have to stoop down for a drink.'

They pissed off uncomprehending and are probably, during lucid moments, still trying to decipher his meaning.

Thade Jeffrey and sons Geoff and Dan, especially Geoff, were excellent fishermen. Geoff, my cousins Hugh and Liam and myself took turns one Good Friday playing a twenty-eight pound salmon for hours while Dan ran to the church to get his father out of the Good Friday ceremonies to bring his net and landing gear.

I learned religion also in Currow. Charlie King, Currow's answer to Murphy International Builders, taught me the Our Father and he hardly knew it himself. I also learned the funniest, most incorrect responses to the old Latin Mass I have ever heard since. So I became an altar boy. With a few other altar 'boyos' I nearly caught fire, or at least my surplice and soutane caught fire, between two rows of candles during the Lenten ceremonies. The 'boyos' — Dennehy, Fleming and Doyle — had polished off a bottle of Morgan's altar wine and only for quick thinking by Fr David Walsh we would have been burned alive.

So all in all, by the time I left Currow for Newbridge, I had had the best preparation any child could have to meet life on any terms.

One major sadness and my first taste of real tragedy had occurred during the previous summer. Dadda Dennehy had died in his sleep and the death of the greatest friend, teacher, coach and companion I ever had left me absolutely stunned and numb. I know that there were many, many people in Currow, the surrounding parishes and further afield who were equally indebted to him in various ways. He was the most generous man of mind and spirit I have ever known. From him I learned real pride, responsibility, self worth, goal-setting, hard work, respect for my fellow man and all the noble things that are the province of human beings.

I was enormously fortunate in the extended family life that I had — it was like having three sets of parents. By the time I got to Newbridge College, in September 1953, there was nothing I couldn't do, academically or in sport. Currow, I will always be in your debt.

The honesty of life, the simple rural honesty of hard work, of farmers bringing their few gallons of milk to the creamery next door, their good-natured animated chat and humorous joking with one another; the going to Mass on Sundays, cycling to Castleisland to meet my parents and my only brother on Saturdays; the freedom to roam the countryside at will and learn from nature. All those things and situations filled me to overflowing with a knowledge of myself, an appreciation of those around me and a freedom to look anyone in the eye without fear, inferiority or equivocation.

There is no doubt that the first dozen years of one's life are the most important and I am fortunate that I spent mine in Currow, Castleisland and Kerry.

3

All Roads Lead to Lynne

*'The difference between a successful person and others is
not a lack of strength, not a lack of knowledge but rather a
lack of will.'*
(VINCENT T. LOMBARDI — FAMOUS AMERICAN FOOTBALL
COACH)

I LEARNED to play rugby at Newbridge College. I learned
my love of the game from my father and my uncle, Bill
Dennehy.

Newbridge College is far from your fashionable rugby col-
lege but despite its very small selection from which to pick
cup-winning teams, it has produced an inordinate number of
Irish rugby players over the past thirty years or so: guys like
Seamus and Frankie Byrne, Fergus Keogh, my brother Tom,
Tony Twomey, Kevin Lavelle, Mickey Quinn, Robbie McGrath,
Tom Grace, Freddy McLennon, Ronan Kearney, myself and
others.

What Newbridge did was to stimulate individual person-
alities, knowledge of the game, the will to win and *never* to
give up, enormous competitiveness and a high degree of
self-motivation. Academically, it gave us the basis of a good
education and prepared us reasonably well for life in the big
bad world. I have nothing but very fond memories of life by
the Liffey in sleepy Co. Kildare in the 1950s.

During my time in Newbridge I made many good friends
among the staff especially Fathers Anthony Delaney and John
Heffernan. Later, two school mates of mine, Paudge Duggan

17

(now deceased) and Jim Harris, joined the Dominican Order and I met them a lot after I had left school life. Johno and Tiddler Delaney helped me to get married to Lynne in Bristol in 1967, baptised my children, and were good friends to me when I needed them.

Newbridge College in 1953 was a far cry from Ranalough National School in Currow with its turf fires and bottles of milk heating in a semi-circle around the hearth. However it was a nice friendly place to me for five lovely years and I adored every minute of it. I achieved every honour the school bestows on its pupils apart from becoming a priest. Indeed, at least two of the white-collared gentry almost chucked me out after Prize Day for taking a local girl to the pictures. What a sin that was! I didn't even hold her hand! Nevertheless, I adored Newbridge and I really hated leaving. I clearly remember crying the whole way to Dublin in the bus on the day I left.

I am deeply grateful for the building materials the Dominicans gave me. It is only as life goes on that I have truly appreciated what good people they were and how genuinely interested they were in all of us and in our futures.

Nowadays, I live in Sherlockstown, about ten miles from the college, and I cycle past, on my Raleigh All Terrain V6 21-gear 4-wheeler, quite regularly. It brings back a flood of almost unbearable nostalgia as well as the odd salty little tear.

During the holidays I always brought home a couple of oval balls — there weren't many rugby balls in Kerry during the 1950s! I spent hours practising the skills with Uncle Bill in Currow behind the creamery and mealtimes with Dad discussing the laws of the game and the options that were open from all hypothetical phases of play.

Dad really taught me how to think about rugby and offered me totally new dimensions on its thought processes. I was introduced to books by B.H. Travers, Bob Scott and others and became an avid reader of J.B.G. (Bryn) Thomas' accounts of Lions tours. After my first visit to Lansdowne Road I was smitten and nurtured a lifelong ambition to represent Ireland.

My Gaelic football background was a tremendous help especially in ball handling and kicking skills as well teaching me to move to the ball instead of waiting for it. The various coaches or trainers in Newbridge taught me how to play prop forward, wing forward, No. 8, scrum half, centre and full back. I preferred playing centre and wing forward, two positions that are quite close in reality. Kevin Kelleher, probably Ireland's greatest referee after Dave Burnett, encouraged me a lot at the Leinster Schools level as did Fr Grace of Terenure College.

In 1958 I went up to UCD to the College of Science to start my pre-vet year and it was at college and through rugby that I met the vast majority of my lifelong friends — Ned Thornton, Brendan Doyle, Jimmy Kelly, Ray McLoughlin, Bill Mulcahy, Kevin Prendergast, Henry Wall, Ted Watson, Pat Casey, P.J. Dwyer, Al Moroney, Brian O'Halloran, Jerry Tormey. The list is endless.

Garryowen was my first senior club and my time there, playing at outhalf with Brian (B.O.F.) O'Farrell at scrum half was probably my first taste of serious rugby. I was extremely fortunate in coming under the wing of Tim McGrath, Tom Nesdale and Tom Coffey. Charlie Mulqueen, John Fahey, Davy and Rusty Keane were just out of short trousers at that time too. I was home for a year's sabbatical from UCD and enjoyed that year immensely with Garryowen. Limerick and Munster rugby hardened me up in all the right places. People like Michael Anthony Francis English were a great help to aspiring young players, as he is now to my son Andrew.

In 1960 I returned to UCD and was extremely fortunate to be around during Henry Wall's last year as club captain. Henry taught us all what commitment, fitness and dedication were about and Dr Jack Moloney, whenever he could tear himself away from his developing medical practice and his lovely Denise, spent hours helping us to become better organised and build a team.

This was the beginning of what was, in my opinion, the most talented, vibrant rugby team with which I have ever been involved. Thank God we had no 'coaches' — we talked it all out among ourselves and gave allegiance to our leader Henry Wall and let him manage and motivate us. Almost all the players in that 1960–65 era played for Ireland and in 1965 Ray McLoughlin, 'Wigs' Mulcahy, Henry Wall and myself played against Scotland and Wales. They were an incredibly gifted bunch of players and fifteen-man non-stop attacking rugby was the hallmark of the period. Years afterwards Ned Thornton and myself introduced some of our 'moves' of the 1960s to Ollie Campbell, Ian Burns and Co., to their obvious amazement.

I can safely say that most of what I have learned about man-management, goal setting, training, strategy, tactics and implementation had its roots in UCD Rugby Club. We received exemplary encouragement from Dr Jamesie Maher, Reggie Spellman, John Blaney, Judge Charlie Conroy, Johnny Geoghegan and Alan O'Grady. Finbar Costelloe was our secretary, Jim Troy our treasurer and Noelie Traynor our fund raiser. Indeed, such was the buzz in UCD at the time that it was expected that first-team players would go on to play for Ireland. In my case, there were a lot of good wing forwards about at the time and it wasn't easy.

I enjoyed my interprovincial rugby during UCD days. Being a Kerryman I opted for Munster, of course. My first game for Munster was against Connaught in Galway and I played in the centre with Paddy McGrath, Jerry Walsh being injured at the time. My next game was against Leinster and even though I was carted off with concussion, we won. I was selected only because either Dave or Paddy Keily or else Liam Coughlan were either too sick to play or not available. However, there was a snag.

There was then, and possibly still is, a large problem between Cork and Limerick when selection for Munster looms every year. Like Brendan Behan said, the first thing on any Irish agenda is the 'split'! At any rate, the Cork-Limerick split was real. I was counted a member of the Limerick camp and so Micky English and Tom Neesdale, two gentlemen and good mates, advised me to opt for Leinster. I did and never regretted it. I knew I was a better open side wing forward than anyone around and that with a fair chance I would get on the Irish team.

Had I not 'declared' my allegiance to Leinster, where I was playing most of my rugby anyway, I know for sure that I probably would not have become even a regular on the Munster team and certainly would never have seen the inside of a green jersey, or a Barbarians or Lions jersey for that matter. I probably would not have coached or even enjoyed rugby to the extent that I did or met the countless rugby friends that I now know.

I owe Leinster rugby and my clubs, UCD and Blackrock College RFC many things and my first club Garryowen for starting me off on the right road.

I am a Kerryman by birth and inclination and I hope to live there soon again, but in rugby I am unashamedly a Leinster man and always will be.

I am indebted also to Desmond Scaife and the Wolfhounds for taking me to Bristol and introducing me to my first wife.

In early September 1963, CMH (Mike) Gibson and myself were the only two uncapped players on Tony O'Reilly's Irish Wolfhounds tour to play Bristol FC and Llanelli RFC.

In that deliciously innocent era, rugby clubs prided themselves on the beauty of their tea ladies and the quality of their after-match teas. Bristol FC was no exception. The Bristol tea ladies XV was coached, captained and managed by one Cicely Grace (Betty) Crabbe. Her tea ladies were a handsome lot — enough to drive a poor 23-year-old Catholic Paddy's hormones into automatic over-drive. At the post match dinner that evening in Fairfax House, being the only non-drinker apart from Gibbo, I was able to allow myself the luxury of checking out the talent at the dance. What a joy it was to have the freedom of the dance floor without being interrupted by your typical male who, despite suffering from mental, visual, verbal and physical brewer's droop, reckons he can 'click' with any bird he wishes.

Anyway, I was squiring this gorgeous, tall lissom Somerset lass called Lynne Thompson around the dance floor in a guaranteed alcohol-free zone thinking what a lovely girl she was and trying to pluck up enough courage to ask her out or in or anywhere she fancied. I smoothly told her my name was Mike, that I was a veterinary student and that I thought she was something else. As I was meandering my way through a Doyle chat-up, my confidence was suddenly shattered by a few well-chosen words delivered from behind me, parallel to my left ear, and directed at my companion.

'His name is Mick' says the voice 'and his father owns half of Kerry.' The O'Reilly had struck again.

Of course he was trying to help me but at the time his intrusion was about as welcome as a dose of herpes in a convent.

Having fought off all comers for the attention of my beloved I learned that she had to go home after the dance, directly mind you, with her aunt, the aforementioned Betty Crabbe. After all, Lynne was barely 17 at the time. Locky Butter offered to 'mind' the aunt for a while. Not to be outfoxed, I asked her to meet me after Mass the following day (Sunday). She replied that she was C. of E., and so she didn't go to Mass. I said that I did and would she meet me? We agreed to meet at the top of Park Street at 12 noon the next day. The 11 o'clock Mass was in Polish, in the pro-cathedral and I left early to be on time. As Paul McWeeney and I met Roly Meates at the top of Park Street afterwards and discussed the joys of having one's own teeth, I suddenly excused myself and said that I had a date with a bird.

I can still register, in my mind's eye, the total incredulity of my companions. I can almost hear Roly saying to himself 'Jesus, a date at 12 o'clock on Sunday morning after Mass!'

Saturday night had been a sleepless one — thoughts and images of Lynne in every conceivable role flashed through my mind in sensual juxtapositions. She had had such a profound effect on me in such a short time, and I had tried so hard to visualise every detail about her that by daybreak I couldn't actually remember what she looked like — a vision without features. However, as she stepped off the bus at the top of Park Street, on that beautiful Sunday morning, I knew instantly that I wanted to look at her lovely face forever. I had lost my heart to her already and could hardly wait to tell her. As she walked towards me in the filtered autumnal sunshine her brown hair glistened and danced about her head.

She was taller than I remembered from the previous night and walked with an erect, confident posture. She was even more vibrant and beautiful in daylight. Her eyes were brown and full of laughter and her face had a rich golden tan that proclaimed her recent holiday in southern France. She wore an open brownish coat, white blouse and grey skirt. I don't remember her shoes but she had fine legs. I thought she was the most beautiful being I had ever met. She had that soft, flirting shyness about her which swelled my breast with love, protectiveness and a fair share of old-fashioned lust as well, I must admit. I adored her from the start and knew that I would ask her to marry me in the not-too-distant future. I could not imagine a life without seeing her every day. The way she talked and laughed and walked and kissed me captivated me entirely. My daughter Sharon reminds me of her now; my daughter Amanda is a mirror-image of me — a much prettier version, thank God. I asked Lynne what she wanted to do for an hour before lunch. She suggested a walk in the park nearby. I would gladly have done a hand-stand atop a bus stop sign for her.

She told me her father had laughed at her when she mentioned her date with an Irish rugby player after 12 o'clock Mass. Admittedly, it wouldn't have been the normal Sunday morning pattern for a well brought-up 17-year-old Protestant girl in dreamy Somerset in the early 1960s. However, to her credit and my eternal gratitude, she kept her word of the night before and turned up as if she wanted to. We've never regretted it either.

Lynne and I sat in a nearby park by a stream for an hour or so talking, kissing and getting to know one another. I probably did all the talking, she the listening. She gave me her address and I gave her my signet ring.

As I put her on the bus for home I had to run down Park Street after it for about a quarter of a mile to return her overcoat. I could imagine what the lads would say, especially as they all knew about this date of mine, had I returned to the hotel with an overcoat. 'You mean you only got her overcoat off in an hour and a half?'

Lynne and I corresponded regularly and we met in London for a few days in January 1964 during a veterinary students' conference. You can bet that I was an absentee vet. I held my own conference.

We didn't meet again until the following July when Lynne came to Ireland for a few weeks' holidays in Kerry. I'll never forget her arrival from Bristol into Cork Airport. My brother Tom and cousin Tom Dennehy were intoxicated with the excitement of it all and afterwards in my Auntie Mai's apartment at dinner, they pole-vaulted up the stairs and cartwheeled around the floor on all fives with passion.

Later we drove to Kerry through some of the most beautiful scenery anywhere in the world but at the time, quite treacherous for driving — particularly Tom Doyle's driving. Cousin Tom worked the handbreak the whole 65 miles home to Castleisland over the mountains. Since my mother's untimely death in 1962 and my father's business relocation to

Co. Kildare there was no regular presence at our old home in Castleisland except when Tom and I were home from university. Doreen Burke (Dodo to all of us — but she was certainly not extinct) looked after us for quite a while after Mammy died.

During that holiday at home with Lynne I got my uncle Bill Dennehy to stay at night in the house in case the neighbours got worried!

I thought too much of Lynne to allow her to be the butt end of understandable gossip in a small town in rural Ireland in 1964, although to give Castleisland its due it was never a typical Irish town and its people were far more Christian and understanding at that time than was the norm. I still have enormous affection for the place. Lynne went back to Somerset to begin therapy radiography at Bristol General Hospital and I went back to UCD to final year veterinary and the captaincy of UCD RFC. A busy year was in store. Lynne and I were corresponding regularly and I had long decided that she was to be my wife. I was friendly with a couple of girls at home in Ireland at the time but my heart and soul was with my absent Lynne. Our next meeting was in London, again for a weekend — UCD were playing London Irish. Lynne travelled up with her Aunt Bet (Cicely Grace to you) and they stayed in a separate hotel from us. I can never thank Bet enough — a gorgeous, spirited woman. Having, as I believed, seen my team off to bed about 11 o'clock on the Friday night I arranged to meet Lynne at her hotel: Ned Thornton (our left wing and one of my oldest friends) thought I was up to something and was waiting for me in the lobby.

To get away to pay court to *mon amour* I had to allow him to piss off on his own — otherwise all the lads would know the score and Doyler's life would have been perilous for the rest of the year as club captain.

We won the game. Lynne and I went to a party with the lads that night in Joe Nesdale's and John McKenna's flat somewhere off the Cromwell Road and spent, since we weren't drinking, a good two hours snogging in a closet under about 100 coats, boots, jock straps and knickers.

I felt like Houdini in reverse that night — a vertitable Paddy O'Romeo with his loins on fire and his rear in gear. We both knew that weekend that we were deeply in love, with an unspoken yet obvious commitment to each other.

We parted at Lynne's train station in tears, utterly heartbroken and pained that we would not be able to meet again until the summer — and this was January. At least Lynne had Bet to cry all over, and she did, on the journey back to Bristol. I couldn't allow myself to be cuddled by Thornton, Ted Watson or P.J. Dwyer on the way back to Dublin. Had I been drinking alcohol at that time I know I would have become totally transmogrified.

In the summer, we won the Leinster Cup for the second year in succession and I failed to pass my exams. I had said to my Dad, Mick the elder, the previous Easter that I couldn't concentrate both on my final exams and the Leinster Senior Cup. I explained that I could repeat the finals in December 1964 and have a better chance of gaining my first full Irish Rugby Cap as well. Without hesitation, he said: 'Well, Micheál, if I were you I'd go for the Cap' and added like a true Kerryman 'but you'd better fucking win it.'

John Hannon, an excellent lecturer and friend (Cork Con of course), now Dean of the Vet Faculty, told me that I had just barely missed passing the final exams and that the college felt I would be better off coming back to repeat for a few months. I owe John and all the staff of the vet college — John O'Connor, Jack Campbell, Dan Collins, Paddy McGeady — a huge debt of gratitude because that decision of theirs actually redirected my whole life. Had I qualified in that summer of '64 I would have become lost in rural Ireland in general vet practice and would never have played international rugby. I would have missed meeting an enormous number of incredible people all over the world and at home who touched me to the heart and unwittingly shaped me into what I was to become and what I am now (a right bollox, I can hear you say).

That summer I spent three romantic, halcyon weeks at Church Farm, Pensford, Bristol with Lynne, Vic and Nibs (Sybil), her parents and her brothers Bruce and Kim (still a brat). We walked every day all over her Dad's farm, 300 picturesque acres in the rolling, hazy hills of Somerset. We sunbathed and swam in the pool at Wookey Hole (Tom King wasn't heard of then); we brought in the hay bales and had ticks all over us. Lynne became golden brown from the sun at Weston, Wookey, Lyme, Bournemouth and Weymouth. My freckles were joining together nicely while the rest of me assumed the usual lobster colour. I got so badly burned in Devon one Saturday that I had to drive back to Church Farm in nothing but my aertex Y-Fronts: a cop in Wells, just by the cathedral, almost had me for indecent exposure till I pointed out that he could have me for over-exposure as well. He saw the humour of the situation and my discomfort and told me to bugger off before he changed his mind.

That was an enchanting time. We articulated our dreams, building our dream house, planning our marriage and betrothed ourselves to each other. Lynne's Dad, Vic, used to lend us his car to drive everywhere — particularly in the evenings — to find the seclusion of the bewitching, leafy bowers that abounded in that part of Somerset, there to conduct our delicious courting rituals and indulge in lovers' small talk and sweet somethings. Many were the times when, lost in each other's arms and dreams, the peaceful heavy breathing silences would be shattered like a rifle crack by little Vic and his ever smaller brother, Uncle Billy, who with lighted flashlights and florid west country visages would jump all over the car shouting 'We caught you, you buggers.'

I could have gladly murdered those two little gobshites many's a time with their ohh, arr, arr . . . 'Twas like trying to get off your mark in a convent. Vic Thompson could have been a veritable human contraceptive device if I had taken any notice of him. A grand man for all that: I love him and Sybil like my own parents.

There's one thing for sure: Billy Jo Spears wouldn't be long grabbing her blanket back up off the ground if she was stalked by Victor Henry and Billy the Kid, and she wouldn't be too safe in the back seat of her ould '57 Chevrolet either.

Lynne had written away to the Catholic Guidance Council for their published leaflets on Catholicism. I was insisting she retain her own faith: she wished to learn about mine. She was a great girl — the most honest and up-front person I had yet met.

In December 1964 I passed my final exams. Ted Watson gave me the good news from the touchline halfway through our UCD game with a Cambridge University XV captained by Mike Gibson. That night I decided with Gibbo to go to Cambridge the following October provided I could get a decent postgraduate course to do.

Life was so sweet that winter. I was in love with Lynne, I had just qualified as a vet and I got my first Irish cap. I had captained UCD and Leinster which had only given me a further taste for the next step. With the consistent support of Dave O'Leary and Dr Gerry O'Reilly, with John Joe White as 'Rugger' giving me plenty of encouragement in *The Irish Press* and the late Paul McWeeney singing my praises in *The Irish Times* I felt I couldn't fail. Dad was a constant source of encouragement all through the difficult times when it often looked like I wouldn't make it. O'Leary, the cute Kerry hoor, said to me after the first trial in 1964, 'Mick, I think you're too small to make the Irish team.' I said I was five feet eleven inches and thirteen stone eight pounds but he dismissed this. His attitude made me mad and I said to myself: 'all right, you bugger, I'll show you who's too small.'

I went out in the final trial and played like a madman and I made it as he knew I would. He was motivating me and I didn't know it. Dave and my old man helped me enormously during my playing career. Dave himself became an Irish selector in 1966 or so. He and Mike Gibson would pull me out of bed at all hours of the night after international matches to discuss points of play, strategy and tactics.

I gained my first cap against France in January 1965. Lynne came over and I was immensely proud of her. Jimmy Nelson and Jack Coffey, both of whom were selectors, made her feel very welcome for her first international rugby match. We were together at all the games that year, in Dublin, Edinburgh and Cardiff.

My first game for Ireland was, I suppose, my most memorable. The preparation was intense and the opposition intimidating. Ray McLoughlin was picked as captain and displayed quite novel thinking in team preparation, concentration and application. His clear, logical mind and his Galway passion was a revelation to those who didn't know him. He was the first captain of real substance to whom most of us had been exposed.

At that time France built most of their play around their back row and half backs and had to be contained there; their lineout men — Dauga and Spanghero — were *tres formidable aussi.*

Ray sent the players off for an hour to think in three groups of five. Ours was 'Noisy' Noel Murphy, Ronnie Lamont, Roger Young, Mike Gibson and myself and we planned our attack and defence strategy.

It was decided and agreed that, as open side wing forward, I should stand out of every scrum on the side opposite their put-in so as to pick up their signals and stop their back row moves early on. It required intense concentration and constant talking to one another to get the timing perfect between the five of us.

The French back row of Lira, Herrero and Michel Crauste was exceptionally strong and committed. Noel Murphy got hold of Lamont and myself in the dressing room before the game and told us the facts of life about international rugby: the pace, the lack of breath and disorientation for the first ten minutes; once we got through the pain barrier we would be alright.

Dave O'Leary had given me poteen to rub into me. I nearly drank it. However, I mixed it with Kennedy's oil of wintergreen instead and began to smell like an alcoholic fitness maniac. Our warm-up was so vigorous we needed to change our gear *before* the match.

Ray squatted with Ronnie Lamont and myself on his back — almost thirty stones. Murphy showered everyone with holy water and apologised to the Protestants. I swore I saw Willie John blessing himself. 'Wigs' Mulcahy was swearing indignities on all 'frogs'. Kennedy was turning himself into a contortionist on the table top. McHale was talking to himself in a corner and Ray was chewing the edge of the table. The backs were in a corner wishing themselves well and trying to pass the ball to each other.

I remember a funny thought passed through my mind. The ball was totally irrelevant if you considered what the French and ourselves had planned to be doing to each other over the next eighty minutes, although I suppose it was handy to have around if you didn't want to get involved in the 'action'.

The kick-off was followed by the most concentrated period of mayhem I have ever witnessed or contributed to. Ronnie Lamont put Herrero almost over the railings with his first tackle; Murphy told Lira that his father was an unknown quantity, while Wigs and Willie John 'dribbled' their counterparts in a footrush for ten yards before realising that the ball had gone into touch. Kennedy was checking the birds in the stand while McHale was trying to forget the birds in the stand and I was trying to land a right cross on Crauste.

During all this Ray was exhorting us to greater effort and castigating us for holding back!

In the first scrum Ray's opposite number stuck two fingers in his eyes, the hooker 'kicked' Wigs on the knee and Murphy chased Lira around behind the posts because Lira had jumped on his hand as the scrum went down. Poor old Gwynne Walters, the Welsh referee, was chasing around in circles.

It was some match. On their put-in I stood out as planned and we wheeled every scrum to the open side — Ronnie and Noisy would detach themselves as Ray shouted, 'left Ireland, wheel', much to the consternation of the French back row and scrum half. When Crauste picked up the first ball of the game to initiate an attack I picked him up and threw him across the top of the scrum to Noisy. Obviously aggression and passion can suddenly produce quite abnormal strength. Like the story, for example, of the all-in-wrestler, the Nagasaki Nip who came to Ireland to fight Ireland's pride and joy, Mickser O'Toole. The Nip had a demon hold called the Nagasaki Scissors which devastated all opponents. After an incredible bout, Mickser came back from the dead to defeat the Nip before an incredulous Dublin crowd. Eamonn Andrews was almost speechless as he related over the wireless how the Nip unexpectedly described a beautiful arc up into the air, landed on his head and was concussed, leaving Mickser barely able to stagger to his feet to accept the applause and the title.

The verbose and imaginative Mickser, with considerable embellishment, described the final seconds of his epic struggle and for the sake of brevity I will cut it short. 'Eamonn a mhic,' says Mickser, 'Yer man the Yid, so solly, the Nip, clapped his scissors on me and it was fierce. My right leg was around the back of me head, me tongue was swelling up, me eyes were bulging and me heart was thumping. I almost fainted and opened one eye. It was then I saw the pair of testicles dangling in front of me eyes and in despair I bit into them; and you know Mister Andrews it's amazing where you get the strength from when you bite into your own bollox!' You know what I mean.

I scored a try in the first half and Christian Darrouy scored his towards the end of the second half, so it was a three-all draw. It was a great tussle and probably a lousy match. We beat Scotland and England that year but succumbed to Wales and Clive Rowlands in our Triple Crown bid. Sounds familiar! We ended the season with a win over South Africa — an historic occasion.

That spring I began to work as a vet at home in Castle-island with Dave Geaney and Jimmy McCarthy. Life was great. Lynne came over and we had a wet, windy and wonderful holiday in Waterville, at Billy Huggard's Butler Arms Hotel. We became engaged and travelled to Dublin, to Weirs in Grafton Street, to buy the identical ring my father and mother had bought there twenty-six years previously. It was an idyllic summer, never to be forgotten. Lynne and I were happy beyond words, as happy as only lovers can be. Lynne also travelled around with me on farm calls and we had hilarious times.

But like everything else, summer ended. Autumn came, bringing a new adventure and a new challenge. In October 1965, I 'went up' to Cambridge.

4

Cambridge — Salad Days and Naughty Nights

'Big fleas have little fleas
Upon their backs to bite 'em,
And little fleas have smaller fleas
And so ad infinitum'
(TIMOTHY RYAN, MATHS TEACHER, NEWBRIDGE COLLEGE, 1955)

IT was on a cold, miserable Sunday evening that I first set eyes on Lucan G. Pratt, in a medieval pub somewhere in the rural time-warp that enveloped Cambridge in the mid-1960s.

He cut a rakish figure as he leaned nonchalantly against the pool table, pork pie in one hand and mug of beer in the other, the pool cue abandoned temporarily on the green baize table. He looked up at my companion and myself and said with a mixture of authority and feigned annoyance, 'What kept you, you silly buggers? I've been waiting for hours.' We made some perfunctory excuses and proceeded to try to beat him at pool for the next two hours — but to no avail. He took pride in being good and in hammering us amateurs.

He was Dr C.L.G. Pratt, Tutor for Admissions at Christ's College, Cambridge. I had applied for entry to pursue a post-graduate degree course and he had arranged this informal tete-a-tete in the pub that Sunday evening preparatory to a much more formal interview in his office at nine o'clock the following morning.

My companion was John H.H. James, of Pendine, Wales, who was then a final year veterinary student. He had driven me all day from Porthcawl to Cambridge across Wales and England to meet Dr Pratt.

I had played for Ireland the previous day against Wales at the Arms Park in our unsuccessful bid to win the Triple Crown. We had disposed of Scotland and England in grand fashion but yet again, Wales was our stumbling block — Wales and that wily old friend of mine Clive W. Rolands. He was more than just a scrum half — he was more like a scrum three-quarters. He didn't like passing the ball, a peculiar trait in a scrum half if ever there was one, but he could kick quickly and accurately in any direction he liked. He did this at every opportunity. He could even kick while lying on his back, thus avoiding the murderous intentions of wing forwards like Budge Rogers, Derek Grant, Noel Murphy and myself. It is said in Swansea that Rowlands invented the 'double bank' at the lineout in 1965 to ensure a more plentiful supply of kickable balls for himself. Anyway I was dejected despite the hilarity of the previous night at the Seabank Hotel when my father and Richard Harris — before his McArthur Park days — and others invented a bottle-throwing contest with a difference. They paid for the drinks, the bottles and the glasses together at each round, poured the gargle into the glasses, drank as fast as they could, set the glasses up as targets and threw the bottles at them. I was a non-drinker at the time and so had to content myself with paying court to my own maiden in a secluded nook somewhere in the hotel — hence the word 'nookey'!

Anyway John and myself traversed Wales and England in a clapped-out Morris Minor that sported wheels as extras and a heater with as much calorific output as a hair drier; the whole car would have needed to be immersed in Lourdes water before being entered for an MOT test. However it got us there eventually and I was delighted to talk for such a long time and cover such a variety of topics with a bloke for whom I have always had special regard. I got a real flavour of Cambridge from our odyssey.

The next time I travelled across Wales and England was in the summer of 1986 as Lions and Five Nations 'coach' in the company of Clive Rowlands and the finest bunch of rugby players you would ever wish to meet — the 1986 Lions. But that's another story.

I spent that Sunday night in a turret in Christ's College, dreaming of Henry Tudor and other ghosts of medieval England after a supper of cold pork pies and coke — a diet calculated to age the brain cells of an Einstein and reduce a normally confident Michael G. Doyle to an incoherent, snivelling hulk by morning. I kept remembering Brendan Behan's poem:

> 'Don't speak of the alien minister,
> Nor his creed without meaning or faith
> For the foundation stones of his temple
> Were the bollox of Henry the Eighth!'

At 9 a.m. sharp, as I entered the private study of my pool-playing pal Dr Pratt, a worn, bald, out-of-shape rugby ball materialised in a descending curve at my head. I caught it easily and a surprised Pratt exclaimed 'You've passed your first test, Doyle.'

'If I had known that,' I replied 'I probably would have dropped the fucking thing.'

He ignored the familiarity and the profanity and elicited from me over the following hour or so my reasons for wishing to join the elite of sporting geniuses that populated Christ's College at the time: the old elite of homosexuals, art custodians and communists had long since departed — probably to MI5.

'Doyle,' he said, 'How do I know that you are not just another Paddy on the make? How do I know you are not just coming up to Cambridge University to get a rugby blue?'

I replied: 'Pratty, old boy, I am a practising veterinary surgeon earning quite a lot of bread which will cease when I come up to Cambridge. I have five international rugby caps for Ireland and I have played for five years for a UCD team of talented players whose girlfriends would beat the living daylights out of every combined Oxford-Cambridge team this decade. Why should getting a blue for Cambridge be that important to me?'

Having explained that I wished to pursue a post-graduate course of studies at my own expense to allow me time to think for myself and to develop some specialisation in animal health, Dr Pratt accepted me and was a serious and helpful friend to me over the following couple of years.

John James arranged that I would stay with him and his mates at the prestigious address of 5, Richmond Terrace, contiguous to Jesus Common, Cambridge's outdoor swimming pool and the Fly and Pecker Pub (or something like that) not to mention a couple of doss houses.

The River Cam, from which Cambridge derives its name, meandered its sleepy course through the beautiful university city just over the wall from our abode.

This was the idyllic place I settled into in October 1965. The prospect of being nearer to Lynne, now that we were engaged, and the challenge of a new course of study, not to mention working with Mike Gibson, who was captain of Cambridge to get the Varsity team into shape, made life very exciting and fulfilling. It resembled Fantasy World by mail order and I enjoyed every single heartbeat of it. Cambridge in the mid-sixties was still very much a charming place. When the student body left during the summer it became very quiet indeed.

I was taking a course in comparative pathology recently established by Drs Gresham and Jennings — a doctor and a veterinary surgeon.

It was quite innovative and I learned a lot from it. All lectures were held from 9 a.m. to 1 p.m. Afternoons were free.

We trained every afternoon for the Varsity XV. My old man attended many of our games and rumour had it that he took in a fair few training sessions as well. There was a full itinerary of games against most of the best rugby clubs in Britain every Wednesday and Saturday until the Varsity game in Twickenham in December.

That era probably signalled the last of the easy-going, free-wheeling students who were all-round sportsmen and could still manage to 'acquire' a degree; around that time the pressure for places, studies and the requirement to pass exams first time round meant that a different calibre of young man was coming up to university — not the right type for the archetypal rugby team. And there were very few old stagers like me. Previously, many men coming back from service in the armed forces 'went up' to Oxford and Cambridge; these guys were well-matured and good sportsmen. They contributed handsomely to the stability and development of younger chaps on various teams. By the mid-sixties this had come to an end and potential Varsity players were so young and inexperienced that Mike Gibson's and my own major fear for the season was diaper rash!

I had spent five wonderful years at UCD as a student and had played with the best players and on the best teams of many a decade from 1960–65. UCD and TCD teams of that period would have hammered any combined Oxford/Cambridge XV. Judge Charlie Conroy had tried to engineer such a fixture but even his resourcefulness was thwarted — God rest his soul and that of his son Paddy. We had our annual Colours match against Trinity in Lansdowne Road every December and they were memorable encounters too. So the Varsity game preparations in Cambridge were nothing new really and I enjoyed them. We didn't have great individual players on the team but we developed into a good side and beat many big-name opponents that season: Newport, Cardiff, Northampton and Bedford. However we only drew with Oxford in the big game. Mike Gibson and Freddy Craig, a Campbell College school mate of Gibbo's and then Oxford captain, cancelled each other out. I had played against Bob Read and John Coker in many Colours matches at home and it was with a considerable sense of deja vu that I met them in '65 playing for Oxford. It was evident that a change of universities hadn't changed any of us. I still early-tackled Bob, as I always had, to unnerve him and make him lose his concentration and I had our team all fired up with fictitious tales of Coker's exploits.

Johnny Coker was a superbly-built ebony black man from Sierra Leone. In 1964 he married a handsome red-haired Irish girl. They made a striking couple in Dublin then. Coker almost became an honorary Irishman. He was a popular figure in rugby circles and an obvious target on the pitch because of his colour, his strength and aggression: it often took three or four men to bring him down.

At one post-Colours match dinner he asked Eddie Thornton, his opposing wing three-quarter, if he would be selected for the Irish team if he declared his availability. Thornton assured him that he would have no problems because he obviously had a lot of Irish blood in him.

'Sure Jaysus,' said Eddie 'your ancestors ate every Irish missionary we ever sent out to your neck of the woods.'

Johnny enjoyed that.

He and Thornton maintained a consistent friendly rivalry on and off the pitch for years which continues to this day. Nowadays, of course, friendship reigns. Many a time during UCD/TCD games Thornton could be overheard telling Coker that he'd give him a 'white eye' if he didn't behave himself. Innocent fun and innocent times long gone by — more's the pity.

The quality of rugby then in Cambridge and Oxford was far less exhilarating but nonetheless whole-hearted and enjoyable. I can remember our training sessions every afternoon and the games at Grange Road — a lovely rugby ground. As is customary, we travelled to see Oxford play Major Stanley's XV at Iffley Road and they came to Grange Road to watch us play a star-studded Mickey Steele-Bodger's XV captained by Tony O'Reilly and sporting Noisy Noel Murphy, Kevin Flynn, Tom Brophy and Dave Rollit, to name a few. Neither Oxford nor Cambridge learned one bloody thing about each other but the tradition is a worthy one and the games are worthwhile.

After the Bodger's game Coker came into the shower to see me before his bus took off to Oxford. We agreed that we were both looking forward to kicking the shit out of each other at Twickenham in a fortnight's time and he said that I would be glad to hear that Bob Read, Oxford's outhalf, was still afraid of his life of me. What an ego tripper I was!

I remember the Varsity match for three things. It was a terrible game. I wrecked my knee trying to steer the ball around Nigel Starmer-Smith (always sounds to me like an old Raleigh bike gear change), or more likely trying to steer Nigel around the ball with my right foot. His left hip won that argument and I experienced my first major rugby injury. My third memory, or rather second nightmare, is of lying on my bed in agony that night with Lynne trying to keep my damaged knee cool while both of us tried to learn from, but still ignore the virtuouso mating rituals from the next bed where a team mate jogged horizontally for the whole night. During one lull in the proceedings, I said to him: 'Full marks, mate, I bet that's the first time you've ever done it for Cambridge, Somerset, Kerry, England and Ireland — all in one night!'

Brian Idris Rees was another friend I won't forget. In civilian life he was a medical student with a leaning towards psychology or psycho-sexual analysis, a great companion and a charming guy. On the field of play he was a veritable pocket version of Brian Thomas — the legendary Cambridge, Neath and Welsh second row — and a Christ's man to boot.

Brian Rees's aggression and commitment were awesome. He played for Wales against us in Cardiff in '67 and was spoken to often by referee Mike Titcomb, a good Bristol man. Eventually Mike became pissed off and called Reeso, Mike Gibson and myself to one side; he warned Gibbo and myself that if we Irishmen couldn't control our mate, the Welsh hooker, he would have to send him off! We gave a recalcitrant Dr Rees a little chat about the situation and the three of us finished out the game still good friends.

I was lucky to share our privileged pad at No. 5 Richmond Terrace with four great blokes — John James, Roger Lavelle (another vet student), Jim Stephenson, a Scottish waif and Tony Kitchin — architecture student and Cambridge right wing. My room was first on the left on the ground floor. It became the 'reception room' and had no furniture, except one bed with three mattresses. Kitch's room was next, then the kitchen. On the next floor was the bathroom, loo, Lavelle's and Stevie's rooms. James, the lord of the manor, had his quarters and launching pad on the top floor.

The 'official' girl friends used to arrive every Friday evening from all over the country to be met by five randy youths. Saturday night in our house saw bare bottoms everywhere disappearing into bedrooms like rabbits. Bedsprings creaked like trampolines in a gym with the world championships in full swing.

Jim Stephenson, a Glaswegian, was a delightful bloke. His extraordinarily varied career included being a PC in Durham, a ladies' underwear salesman in Birmingham and an encyclopedia salesman in the midlands. He was fired as a driving instructor in Cambridge when the L-plate firm found out that he couldn't drive very well himself. When I met Jim, he had a job with Reed Corrugated, a company reputedly founded by Michael Anthony Francis English and J.P. Horrocks-Taylor. Jim's worldly possessions, apart from the clobber he wore, were a superb record player and the best collection of Elvis Presley and classical music LPs I have ever seen. He also had a pick-up truck somewhere which he regularly abandoned — it was referred to funnily enough as 'The Boomerang'. He was an amazingly gifted fellow but his talents were either too way out to commercialise or they were just plain daft.

At the end of a Friday night pub-crawl Jim had a regular routine. He would wend his way to Jesus Common, a wide open green space, take off all his clothes and ride one of the grazing horses bare-backed and bare-arsed around the Common; he would then put his clothes back on, gain access to the outdoor municipal swimming pool and swim for half an hour or so fully clothed. Afterwards he would amble back to the house and further live out his fantasies. In the kitchen he would turn off all the lights, open all windows, light about twenty candles in two or three candelabras, put on a classical LP at full volume and with a kitchen fork brandished like a baton he would conduct the orchestra and 'bring in' every instrument like a seasoned conductor. While all this would be going on, a frying pan full of frying rice would be lepping up and down on the gas cooker! If ever a man knew how to make a mess in a kitchen, it was Jim Stephenson. He was certainly one of life's characters who made my sojourn at Cambridge a memorable one.

Roger Lavelle was a vet student and hailed from Lancashire. A big blonde, handsome bloke, he was a softie when it came to women — like someone else I know very well. If Roger's girlfriend didn't turn up some weekends he would go on the piss and arrive back at No. 5 in the most amorous, inventive mood imaginable. While the rest of us were tucked up in bed he would pretend out loud that he had seduced the most superb girl into coming home with him and he would proceed to chat her up and invent two-way conversations for hours on end. He was another performer and kept us entertained for hours, days and weeks. I believe he is in Australia now. I hope he is successful.

John James was studying for final vet and was travelling to Cardiff at weekends to play rugby. He had no steady girlfriend that year. However, he was the master of the shitty grin and the prototype poser when it came to women — he roped in his fair share all the same.

While at Cambridge Brian Idris Rees made the acquaintance of one Miss Sarah Kipling of Leamington Spa and I am glad to report they are still man and wife. Brian and I were almost inseparable at Cambridge and I really missed him when I left.

I last met him in 1989 on the bridge in Cardiff beside the Angel Hotel — Fergus Slattery and myself had been interviewed by BBC Wales and had to sing 'Sospan Fach'. Rees came along with his charming daughter and embarrassed the hell out of me — and that is some feat.

I travelled regularly to Church Farm in Somerset, Lynne's home, on weekends when she couldn't travel to Cambridge. At that time, 1965, it was some drive on a Saturday evening after a game — five-and-a-half hours across country. It was just as bad coming back on Monday mornings.

However, it is a drive that is forever etched in my memory. It's through some of the most beautiful countryside in the world — Cambridgeshire, Bedfordshire, Buckinghamshire, Oxfordshire, Gloucestershire and Somerset. It was the most carefree and happy time in my 25 years on earth up to that point.

Academically, I laid the groundwork for my later veterinary specialisation and business pursuit — animal health programming. Cambridge gave me breathing space and time to think as well as helping me to shape my life. It also gave me unforgettable memories of people, places and events. Even as I write, evocative reminiscences flood into my mind. I captained a Cambridge Catholics XV in full Varsity jerseys, courtesy of Gibbo, against an Oxford XV captained by Ollie Waldron. Lynne was our touch judge while Tommy Bedford, the great South African number eight, from Durban, ran the line for Oxford. The ref won the day.

I was leader of a Cambridge University boxing supporters' bus load that travelled to Oxford in March to a Colours boxing match. John Rush, a bearded colossus, was the Cambridge heavyweight, and I had been asked to help him psychologically in his bout against John Coker who had been the Sierra Leone middle weight at the Tokyo Olympics. (He couldn't get gloves to fit him so hadn't boxed in that Olympics). I told him that Coker was vulnerable to crowding and verbal abuse. John Rush was at one time the Yardbirds road manager or something like that. He cut quite a figure in his boxing silks: unfortunately it wasn't the figure of a boxer.

After a poser of a first round full of grunts, farts and snarls, the bell for the start of round two signalled a do-or-die attack from our hero. He pounded across the ring like an elephant, kneed Coker in the testimonials and almost head butted him out of the ring to instant disqualification — much to his own relief and ours. He said he'd been pissed off dancing around with the coloured bloke and wanted to get to the bar. I think we won the rest of the contest and came home happy.

Cambridge was my wonderland and Lucan Pratt, Windsor Lewis, Mike Gibson, Mickey Steele-Bodger, Kenny Webb, Brian Rees, John James, Denis Gathin, Dai Evans and all the other wonderful people I met there were of huge significance in my life, a life which would have been emptier, poorer and much less complete had they not touched it, however briefly. I am proud to have been there, grateful for the experiences and the stimulation and ever mindful of the people and the memories. Up Cambridge. G.D.B.O.!

5

Marriage and the Lions

'Guide me, O though great Jehovah,
Pilgrims through this barren land
I am weak but thou art mighty
Hold me with thy powerful hand.
Bread of Heaven, Bread of Heaven,
Feed me 'till I want no more
Feed me 'till I want no more.'
(WELSH HYMN, LIONS TOUR SONG SHEET,
   SOUTH AFRICA 1968)

ALL the time I was in Cambridge Lynne had been taking instruction from Monsignor Hughes and Fr Rodgers in Bristol so that she would know what a burden it would be to marry an Irish Catholic. Her vicar had advised her Mum, Sybil, that Lynne should become a Catholic. I wished her to remain C. of E. She was a stubborn lady, even then. In the end, as she said herself, 'Mick, there is no earthly reason why I should not join your church. I have no antagonism towards it and I am happy to be at one with you.' When she made her first confession and communion I fully realised the commitment she was making to me and I was often afraid that I might not be up to her standards. I went into confession before her that evening and told the priest the story about Lynne and asked him to take it easy on her for her first confession! Anyway, he put her through the ropes and extracted from her a list of sins she'd never committed. Having given her a wheelbarrow full of prayers to say as her penance — two full rosaries to

44

my three Hail Marys — he told her to look after me properly and then escorted her laughing from the confession box. She thought that we were all mad. She was right!

In true male chauvinistic style the wedding date had to coincide with a suitable non-rugby weekend. As it happened however, we were wed on the Saturday of a double representative interpro game at home. Ned Thornton was the only rugby friend from Ireland able to travel but all my relatives and close friends turned up, thank God. We were married in the Pro-Cathedral in Bristol in November 1966. Monsignor Tom Hughes and friends from Newbridge College days, Fr John Heffernan and Fr Anthony Delaney, tied the knot for us. It was very ecumenical — the left-hand side of the church was all Prods and the right-hand side all Papes.

We honeymooned in Torremolinos for a windy fortnight in November. We had a nice time without ever hitting the high spots or getting our names on the orgasmic Richter scale! This particular Paddy confesses that it was frightening for him to realise that at the very moment both people said 'I do' he was transported from a snivelling, guilt-ridden self-conscious randy single man into a raving sex maniac with a game licence who was exhorted to procreate henceforth like bunnies in Ballybunion.

I personally found the transformation to married life too sudden and it took me a while to settle down to what might be regarded as normality. I'm sure Lynne wondered at times what kind of 'eejit' she had married but I was too afraid, too proud and too thick to admit anything to my peers or seek help. Marriage actually scared me and I was shocked to realise that I hadn't a clue how to cope. At that time Lynne was a mere 20-year-old and I was a slip of a lad at 26.

Lynne got a job in Edinburgh as a therapy radiographer. She had qualified in first place with distinction two weeks before we were married. I played for a season with Edinburgh Wanderers where I enjoyed superb rugby, especially down in the Borders. Ever since then, I have the utmost regard for Scottish rugby. They play with a flair and precision that we lack.

Lynne and I assiduously practised the rhythm method, the Billings method, the Eskimo method, the swinging from separate chandeliers method and every daft non-contraceptive method imaginable to delay a family until we could settle down and get to know one another properly. We took our own temperatures, the landlady's, neighbours' wives', local female cats' and dogs' to ensure that no female was ovulating within eight inches of me at any one time!

Happily nothing worked and Lynne became pregnant with Andrew. He was thought of in Kerry, conceived in Scotland of Irish and English parents and one set of Scottish grandparents. But he would be born a Doyle in Ireland and in due course he was, thank God, in Mount Carmel Hospital with the help of Karl Mullen and the late Dr Paddy Swan, in November 1967. Sybil, Dad, Dave O'Leary and myself got gloriously pissed.

As an aside, while I can understand the logic and physiological fine print of the safe period or natural method - call it what you will — I cannot accept the psychological turmoil that denying a natural physiological process entails. I will explain: female mammals, including humans, experience high and low fertility periods at regular intervals throughout any year during their reproductive lifetime. Nature, working through physiological stimuli called hormones, ensures that at the time of highest fertility there is a correspondingly high sexual desire or acceptance of overtures; conversely, at times of least fertility — the 'safe' period — sexual desire is at its lowest. What proponents of the safe period are saying in effect to a woman is: 'You can have all the sex you want when you least desire it but you can't have intercourse when you most want to unless you want to become pregnant.'

That is the nub of it. It is wholly unnatural and creates the most incredible mental anguish. That fine distinction between the laws of nature and the Natural Law becomes blurred into oblivion when two people in love are steamed up within inches of each other. Self-denial me arse!

Anyway, thank God it didn't work for us and we wouldn't have had Sharon either at the time we did in March 1969 — almost nine months to the day after I returned from the Lions tour of South Africa. She was a most welcome little Missy. Up Billings; up after you! I bet if we had women clergy, who understand nature more completely than men, our friend Billings would have been strung up by the balls long ago and 'condomised' for ever.

I went off to tour Australia with Ireland in May/June 1967. We had beaten them in Dublin in January and we repeated the exercise in Sydney in May and again in October 1968 when I played my last representative rugby match. Coincidences are a funny phenomenon — they probably have some meaning which eludes me. For instance, my first and last games as Irish coach were against Australia 1984 and 1987. Also, I played on the winning Irish team in Cardiff in 1967 and I coached the first Irish team to win there in 18 years in 1985.

Australia in 1967 was a lovely country and incredibly new. The people were superb and their rugby players talented, athletic, abrasive and aggressive. But they were good sports. It was the first tour undertaken to Australia by an International Board country and was a howling success — on and off the field! Eugene O'D. Davy and Des McKibben were manager and assistant manager respectively and each had an excellent rapport with the players. Dr Jamesie Meagher travelled at his own expense and looked after all our medical problems: he was in constant demand.

Irish players of all eras had subscribed to a fund to send Charlie McCorry, our beloved baggage man, on the trip with us; Dazie Clarke and Collie Smith's Dad also travelled as well as Fred Cogley, or Fled Cogrey as the Japanese call him, and Paul McWeeney. Ian Cairnduff came along as well for the craic.

The rugby was good and the social life even better. I've never been in more Irish clubs in my life, including the Pink Pussy in King's Cross in Sydney. We spent a wild night in New York on the way out. Willie John, Jerry Walsh and myself were invited to leave a pub called the Red Hand for singing too loudly. We spent half a day in San Francisco Airport drinking Tom Collinses and talking cowboy talk. The Waikiki Hotel on Waikiki Beach in Hawaii was our base for a couple of days and we nearly lost Phil O'Callaghan and Terry Moore to two dark-skinned Wahines.

We called into Nandi Airport in Fiji for a few drinks before landing in Sydney. After a civic reception, we flew to Brisbane and after half an hour's rest we turned out to train. Train — what a joke! Jamesie had almost to perform a tracheotomy on Paddy McGrath — he went into oxygen debt and couldn't breathe. But somebody loosened his jockstrap and he returned rapidly to normal. I met him recently and he still claims that it was exercise-induced bronchospasm!

It was a memorable tour. Coming home via Hong Kong, Singapore, Teheran, Athens, Rome, London, Dublin and Glasgow by air and train from Glasgow to Edinburgh was also memorable in its own way! It was the first and probably the last time for me to have my confession heard or rather beaten out of me in a hotel room in Hong Kong.

The most memorable part of it was Lynne and our unborn Andrew waiting on the platform for me at Haymarket Station, Edinburgh. Our six week separation had naturally made us more aware of what we meant to each other and our lives took on a keener edge and a newer depth. Tony O'Reilly had told me a long time earlier that a rugby tour cleanses the spirit. I now knew what he meant. It lays a few ghosts to rest as well. We could have split up at any time between January and May 1967. The six weeks absence in Australia allowed us both to get a new perspective on each other and on our commitment. It helped to focus our minds on things that mattered.

I broke my leg in July playing soccer at Murrayfield to keep fit. Lynne and I returned to Ireland in August 1967, her Dad driving the car, with us and our belongings – plus two crutches.

I began training in September in Belfield and Eddie Downey who had his physio practice in the Montrose Hotel put a lot of work into getting muscles and limbs into fighting shape. I enjoyed many a chat and a joke with actors Joe Lynch and Eddie Golden who shared the sauna with me around that time. Joe was a fund of stories about rugby in Cork in the 1950s. Both were great company in a sauna. Pity it didn't have a bar. I began to play for Blackrock College in November and was picked to play in the first trial in December when I pulled a bloody hamstring.

I was selected for the Probables in the final trial; Mick Hipwell and Ken Goodall completed our back row. Noel Murphy, Gerry Culliton and my brother Tom made up the Possibles back row. An intriguing game was in the offing. My hamstring was not fully healed and Dave O'Leary had told me on no account to come off the pitch with a hamstring injury! Very early on of course it 'went' and severely restricted running, especially my speed off the mark.

I hung around 'off side' for most of the day to Johnny Moroney's annoyance and had fun with Noisy Murphy. He was trying to engage Tom and myself in a row: I was trying to brazen it out and tell him that I was assured of my place. Towards the end of the first half Mike Gibson put up a high kick ahead which was followed by Alan Duggan and myself, albeit ponderously. As luck had it the Garryowen prop, Mervyn O'Connor was getting up from an injury in a previous ruck and ran into me. At last my opportunity! I put on a dazzling display of concussion and was carried off on a stretcher. I can still see Noisy dancing around shouting 'Ref, he's codding us, don't mind him.' I waved Noisy a weak goodbye from my bed of pain as I was shepherded through the stile and into the medical room under the stand. Niall

Brophy said to Davo, 'I don't think he should go back on' to which Davo replied, 'You can be bloody full sure he won't.'

Dr Jamesie Meagher concurred and I recovered with two large brandies. I got showered and dressed and returned to watch the second half. Billy O'Mahoney had replaced me and there was a royal competition for places: they knew I was a certainty now — my hamstring had held up! So they were fighting for one place, Tom, Noel and Billy. However, Mick Hipwell got it with Ken Goodall at No. 8 against France in Paris.

Noisy was obviously impressed by my 'concussion' and was inspired to copy it against Wales in 1969 in Cardiff when Brian Price had a few words with him. In 1967, Noisy had collected a boot in the jewellery, allegedly from the same source, and had been carried off in agony. I took over the pack leadership and decided that the Welsh No. 4, Ben Price, was the culprit. I exhorted our forwards to spend the next ten minutes 'getting' him — especially Phil O'Callaghan, Willie John McBride and Mick Molloy.

Mike Titcomb, the Bristol referee and a friend of mine, overheard me and called me to one side. 'Moike' says he. 'Oi 'eard that and Oi don't like it, see.' Accidentally on purpose, I took this warning to mean that if we didn't sort things out very quickly — like within five minutes — we wouldn't be let sort them out at all. We did, too, and when the bould Noisy saw Brian get a bit of a hammering he forgot about the injurious insult to his testimonials and came bounding on to the pitch looking for action. We won at a canter, 5–3.

Paris in 1968. Stade Colombes was beautiful, but the match was filthy. Early on in the first half Ken Kennedy had his cartilage 'kicked' out and Mick Molloy had his fibula broken. Mick Hipwell had to go in at loose head prop and Ken Goodall into the second row with Willie John. Syd Millar went in hooker and Phil O'Callaghan at tight head prop. So we were down to six men and the game of rugby was forgotten.

Survival was the order of the day and there was no way that eight Frogs were going to beat six Paddies — no fucking way! I admit that as pack leader I was incensed at their filthy, sneaky play and exhorted our pack to let the bastards have it at every single opportunity. War was declared.

The referee was Larry Lamb. He called me aside and said; 'As an old Cantabrian, Doyle, I'm disappointed in you. However,' he said, 'I know they're doing it but I can't catch them.' I pretended not to hear Larry too well, a plausible enough thing to do in a noise bowl like the Stade Colombes, and we continued to get our retaliation in first as often as we could get away with it. We lathered the bejasus out of the French pack at the slightest provocation and we almost won as well. Larry Lamb, a fine referee and a genial man, kept a good grip on us all.

This was no Brian Price/Noel Murphy spur-of-the-moment incident. Some of these French players were dangerous in my opinion. On a straight one-to-one face-to-face, they wouldn't stand up to you. Well, that day six Paddies put manners on them. I would love to take them on with eight dirty players but I couldn't find that many in Ireland. For all that, the French are gifted, exhilarating rugby players and most of them are decent blokes.

At the dinner that night I was approached by Dave O'Leary, Des McKibben and Noel Henderson. They were discussing the selection of my brother Tom at wing forward. I pointed out that it was illogical because our back row didn't have a chance with all the injuries and no substitutes. However, Mick Hipwell was wrongly dropped and Tom Doyle was selected. I was sorry for Mick and I think his non-selection was a mistake and wrong. Of course I was delighted to have my brother playing for Ireland with me — it is a unique and uncommon honour for two brothers to represent their country at the same time and in similar positions. Tom played against England, Scotland and Wales in 1968. He was an excellent ball player and was game to try anything. He had a quick, fiery temper like me and made his presence felt around the pitch. He deserved a lot more caps but he didn't really stick at it long enough or work hard enough at it. He was a good reader of the game and would have made an excellent coach. He had won an All Ireland Gaelic Minor (under 18) medal with Kerry and had good football instincts and skills. I always felt that he was a better ball player than me but I probably worked harder at my game and listened more to worthwhile advice.

In the summer of 1968 I went to South Africa with the Lions for the last of the 'fun' tours, as Barry John called it. We won 15 of 16 provincial matches, drew one Test and lost three. South Africa's Test side was stronger than ours, especially in the pack, and their backs were more experienced and harder. We had quite a lot of young players at the start of their careers — for example Barry John, Gareth Edwards and Gerald Davis and our pack wasn't strong enough physically or mentally.

South Africa had some great players then: Frik du Preez, Dawie de Villiers, Jan Ellis, Tommy Bedford, Jannie Englebrecht, Mannie Roux, Tiny Naude, Gys Pitzer, Hannais Marais and others.

They were well coached by Johann Claassen who got them to utilise their strengths against us. The provincial sides, apart from Northern Transvaal, were not great then but their commitment to South Africa and their passion for rugby made them the most formidable foe in international rugby and I am including the great power of New Zealand in that.

Ronnie Dawson, was coach and Tom Kiernan was captain. He was quite a good captain too. David Brooks was the manager of that tour and he certainly left his mark on us and on South Africa.

Ronnie Dawson had been an equally good captain in his day and was an excellent 'thinker' and organiser of coaching courses. To his eternal credit he kept us all out of trouble in South Africa on that tour — especially when the party divided mischievously into the 'wreckers' and the 'kippers'. He is also a man of principle.

The 'kippers' were generally those who slept a lot and alone and included in their number were the more conservative and sober-minded. Ronnie Dawson headed the list which would embrace guys like Delme Thomas, John Pullin, Mike Coulman, Keri Jones, Maurice Richards, Yogi Bear (Syd Millar), Gerald Davies, Billy Raybould, Peter Stagg, Bob Taylor and Roger Arneil, Mike Gibson and Jim Telfer. Mercifully the 'wreckers' were fewer in number and I was one of them.

The 'wrecking', of course, was minimal and mostly self-inflicted. The train that took us from Jo'burg to Skukusa Camp in the Kruger Park for a few days rest got a bit of a battering. A few fire extinguishers were lost through windows which happened to be closed at the time and a few old ladies were inadvertently turfed out of bed by a genuine mistake.

The following morning we woke up to a shattering silence, all we could hear was the menacing, daring, gravelly growl of the odd lion, and the mating calls of assorted wilde-beest and giraffes. Also, we were not moving. Various half-naked ladies gingerly descended from the train on to the narrow gauge tracks to investigate. Our carriages had been disconnected and we had been left about half a mile from the bloody station! Savage attacks from enraged wild animals nagged our sleepy yet fertile awakening imaginations and we got dressed and out of that train at the double.

We had a lot of good-natured fun on that tour and it was a very happy group. We enjoyed a magical couple of days by the river where once the craft carrying Vivien Leigh and Humphrey Bogart had passed during the filming of *African Queen*.

The tour itinerary was fairly ridiculous — changing from sea level to the altitude of the high veldt with astonishing rapidity. We had a major journey by air every Sunday, a 'dry' day on South African flights. However by managerial decree the players brought a couple of bottles of wine each and Brookie brought the cheese. Often, after these aerial cheese and wine parties a few of us — in fact many of us — would be a bit 'bewildered' getting off at the point of destination and some of Brookie's speeches acknowledging words of welcome from our hosts were memorable.

I remember one hilarious speech of his on our arrival at Upington, a one-horse town then, on the Orange river and at the edge of the Kalahari desert. Our new liaison man, a local genial bank manager with a booming voice, appropriately called Jack Horn, welcomed us and said a few words before introducing the mayor who owned an equally prepossessing voicebox (O'Shea christened him Fog Horn). Brookie smiled benignly at the assembled female lovelies lining the walls of the reception room and when his turn came to speak he thanked the mayor for his kind words and referred deferentially to the 'lovely wall flowers just lying around waiting to be flucked' (he did mean plucked?) and added: 'And we are the men to fluck them!'

Brookie was a great guy and we all loved him. He had an infectious air of mischievousness about him which often almost got us into trouble, but which bound all the players to him. Dawson was the ideal foil for him and the two made a great management team. Every Sunday we had a court session with Judge O'Shea on the bench. Gerald Davies was the prosecutor and Syd Millar, the fine and debt collector. It was always quite an occasion. Tess O'Shea would arrive from his rooms suitably attired: a laundry bag for a wig, open dressing gown and a jock strap turned back to front, exposing his gavel. He was some sight as he progressed through the hotel lobby accompanied by Gerald, Syd and various acolytes on his way to the team room.

Everyone had to attend court sessions and answer totally fictitious charges laid against them by other players. Maurice

The infant Doyler.

Aunt Mai (left) with my mother, shopping in Dublin in the 1940s.

My mother and her father Tom Dennehy at Riverside, Currow, Co. Kerry, about 1936.

The 2A class, Newbridge College, 1953.

My mother and father on their wedding day, February 1940.

Confirmation, June 1952.

UCD colours team of 1960. Four of the pack—Wigs Mulcahy (back row, fourth from the *, Henry Wall (with ball), Ray Mc Loughlin (front, second from left) and myself (front, —played for Ireland against Wales and Scotland in 1965.

Conferring Day at UCD, 1965. I have just been awarded my veterinary degree and I'm standing on the college steps with my Dad.

CHRIST'S COLLEGE,
CAMBRIDGE.

27 July 1965

My dear Michael,

　　Thank you for your letter of 13 July. It may
amuse you to know that I had a little trouble securing
agreement as to the proper form to ask you to fill in,
because of the odd nature of your status here. However,
the authorities seem to feel that all we need ask you
to do is to complete (more or less) the form I enclose
herewith and that will be an end to formalities. You
will get a bundle of formal papers from my office during
the next week or so, some of which may interest you but
you will find nothing formidable among them. In the
meantime, I can tell you that College and University
fees are going to amount of £75 per term. The only
other expenses you will have to face will be those of
normal cost of living.

　　I must ask you to let me have your degree
certificate (returnable to you) for matriculation
purposes. There is no hurry about it and you may, if
you wish, bring it with you when you come up in October.

　　With all good wishes.

　　　　　　　　Yours sincerely,

　　　　　　　　C. L. G. Pratt

M. G. Doyle Esq. M.R.C.V.S.
Killarney Road
Castleisland
Co. Kerry
Ireland.

A wonderfully laid-back letter from Lucan Pratt, the summer before I went up to Cambridge

cap. Ireland v. France at Lansdowne Road in 1965. (Back row, left to right): Ken Kennedy,
...asey, Ronnie Lamont, Bill Mulcahy, Willie John Mc Bride, Noel Murphy, Ken Houston.
...ed left to right): Kevin Flynn, Tom Kiernan, Charlie Harte (Pres. IRFU), Ray Mc Loughlin
..., Jerry Walsh, Mick Doyle, Sean Mc Hale. (Ground): Mike Gibson, Roger Young.

...bridge University XV versus Mickey Steele-Bodger's XV, 1965. In the middle of a
...xy of stars, I'm eighth from the left in the middle row.

Gareth Edwards of Wales about to pass the ball in the 1968 international at Lansdowne Ro
That's me on the left and brother Tom on the right.

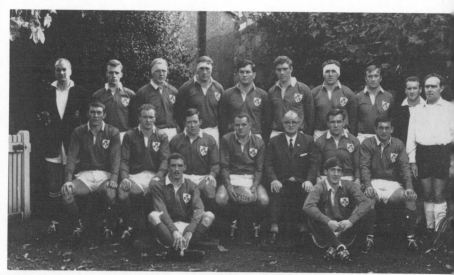

Last cap. Ireland v. Australia at Lansdowne Road in 1968.

Richards, for example, was regularly accused of 'not breaking enough glass' during the previous week. He was fined
two rand (£1) and forced to hurl glasses at the wall for his
penance. Of course there were often more extreme forms of
sentencing. At this time, the Rhodesian crisis was in full
swing. Ian Smith was the white Prime Minister of Rhodesia
(now Zimbabwe) — I wonder what they call the Rhodesian
Ridgeback dog now — who had made the unilateral declara-
tion of independence from Britain in order to preserve white
minority rule. The British Prime Minister, Harold Wilson,
had slapped economic sanctions on Rhodesia and generally
tried to ostracise the Smith regime. The Lions were due to
play a match up there and sanctions or no sanctions we were
able to fulfil the fixture.

Our few days in Salisbury were lovely. We beat Rhodesia
easily and Tess O'Shea scored an hilarious try, injuring
himself in the process. Describing his score to Ian Smith at a
post-match cocktail party he had the Prime Minister doubled
up with laughter. When Smith asked him how he acquired
his injury Tess replied that he had deftly beaten the full back
with a beautiful body swerve but for some inexplicable reason
he then side-stepped back into him in the act of scoring,
thereby injuring himself.

Kiernan and McBride were told late one afternoon that
one of the party had a WOMAN in his room who wasn't his
wife! Having failed to talk their way into the room or to elicit
any response from the occupant, they began to dismantle
the door bit by bit to the delighted astonishment of the
coloured hotel staff, but not of the white lady overseer of the
first floor. She called the police and informed Willie John
and T.J. Willie asked innocently, 'Will there be many of them?'
as he continued to take the door apart. The timing was exquisite. They had gained entry to the empty room just as three
Rhodesian policemen and assorted yelping, howling police
dogs emerged from the lift. Of course, one of the policemen

was a Corkman and a mate of Kiernan's. The cops, Tommy and Willie John, adjourned to the bar while the dogs drank milk from the policemen's helmets. It was some sight.

There was an informal kind of apartheid in Rhodesia but nothing like the dehumanising, institutionalised system that had been introduced to South Africa. I knew very little about apartheid when I went out there.

South Africa was a lovely country in 1968, but coming from Ireland I found the colour divide almost incomprehensible. The Afrikaaners distrusted outsiders but were nice people once you got to know them. They were quite anti-British, particularly in areas around Jo'burg because of their memories of POW camps during the Boer War. Naturally, being Irish established an immediate empathy with people and I don't mean that in any anti-Brit, disparaging way. It was simply a fact of life.

In fact, being Irish is a help anywhere, with the possible exception of being lumped in with that murdering group of despicable people who arrogantly but mistakenly presume to speak for and represent the Irish people — the IRA of every shape and colour.

We were once invited, in Cape Town, to a Cape coloured musical evening. We were the only whites there apart from the Minister of Sport. I had a date with a lovely girl I had just met in Mossel Bay, the charming Avril, so I left the musical appreciation to the lads.

The minister's chauffeur, a romantic chap to his fingertips, drove me in the state Mercedes, bedecked with flags and emblems, to the home of my lady friend and certainly impressed the bird and her neighbours.

On rugby tours, fit rugby players are away from home and from their loved ones for extended periods of time. Even in a group of thirty-two, life gets very lonely and understandably female companionship is essential on these trips. Some blokes can do without the company of a girl, others cannot.

I succumbed when I met the beautiful Avril and spent a lot of time with her during the tour. I almost lost my head as well as my heart and were it not for friendly help and advice from Keith Savage, the Northampton wing three-quarter, I might have been tempted to make an irrevocably wrong decision at a crucial time in my life. I formed a very powerful attachment to Avril over the fourteen weeks or so in South Africa. On the journey home my emotions were bombarded by a number of letters she had written to me and which were handed to me in sequence by one of the air hostesses. She knew I would go home but asked me to remember her love like the dew on the grass. I have done so ever since. She married a few years later and now lives happily in America. On a visit to Britain four years ago she made telephone contact and we had a long, nostalgic chat on the phone. She was my sunshine girl and I pined for years for her after I came home in 1968. Even though Lynne didn't know it, it did affect our married relationship for a while after I returned from that tour. O'Reilly and his cleansing of the soul! Lynne was a great girl. She said before we went on tour that she knew that I was going to meet girls everywhere. She told me to respond as I wanted but asked me not to tell her about it when I returned home. I did both and don't regret it.

My little Sharon, Missy to me, was born about nine months later as if to copperfasten our relationship and mutual respect. She was followed by Amanda, (Ami Jo), three years later. I don't know what I would have done without them. I equally could not have done without Lynne and Andrew in July 1968. Life certainly puts one to the test from time to time. It keeps us all on our toes like the monks and the six foot nun.

I was totally fed up with rugby when I came back from South Africa. I played against Australia and retired at the age of 28 in October 1968. I wanted to develop my professional and business life and I had had a good innings at my sport.

Dave O'Leary brought me out of self-imposed rugby exile in 1973 to play for Blackrock 3rd Es against Terenure. I became very fit in the summer of 1973, began to play seriously for Blackrock First XV and captained them to the Leinster League Trophy shortly after.

Fergus Slattery asked me to coach his team which I gladly did. I began to coach and play for Naas RFC at the invitation of my friend Michael O'Neill and would have slipped quietly and unobtrusively into rugby nostalgia were it not for a phone call one morning from my great friend Victor Brophy who as president of Blackrock RFC, congratulated me on becoming the club's nominee for the Leinster selection committee. I became a sub-selector in 1977 with Ian Cairnduff, the year he was president of the Leinster Branch, and Leinster coach the following year.

Were it not for my club, Blackrock College RFC, I would never have come out of rugby anonymity or taken up coaching. Their unselfish and unflinching support for me from the day I first joined the club at the suggestion of Austin McMahon and Dave O'Leary, gave me a base and the confidence to progress as I did.

I ended my playing career in Belfast in 1980-something playing for a Mike Gibson invitation Lions XV against a crowd of Campbell College drop-outs to celebrate the opening of the Michael Gibson recreation hall. Way back in 1964 I had captained an invitation XV against Ken Kennedy's Irish Universities XV to open Fox's Field, also at Campbell College.

So Campbell College — you started me and you finished me. Thanks for nothin'.

6

Married Life

'The quality of a person's life is in direct proportion to their commitment to excellence, regardless of their chosen field of endeavour.'
(VINCENT T. LOMBARDI, AMERICAN FOOTBALL COACH)

BRINGING up two young ones was naturally the same strain for us as for countless other couples around the world. Moreover, two years of study at Cambridge and Edinburgh had severely depleted our coffers. I came home to work for the family business.

Back in 1953 my father had set up Doyle's Hatcheries Ltd. Using the existing poultry breeding stock developed at Ballyhaise Agricultural College he had built up a very successful breeding and hatching business. In 1956 he set up Irish Poultry Industries Ltd at Kill, Co. Kildare, on a sixty-acre farm which has been the site of Goff's Bloodstock Agency since 1976. He imported 'foundation' breeding eggs from the USA and set about developing the Irish poultry industry. He established breeding farms in different parts of the country.

My father was a visionary, an innovator, a teacher and a dreamer. He developed the poultry industry almost from nothing and taught a lot of people a lot of things along the way. He himself never really reaped his just rewards, a fact acknowledged by many who were associated with him in the early days. Being a visionary, he needed a good business associate to control him, something he has often regretted not having. He taught me so much, especially the value of thinking things out in an unorthodox — but still logical — way.

59

Though in his seventies, he still possesses an incredibly inquiring, lively mind and can even be a pain in the arse at times, especially when you begin to feel smug about yourself.

By the time I arrived back from Scotland in the late 1960s, the family business was contracting because the major poultry groups had developed their own breeding and hatching enterprises. The demise of the independent hatchery was in sight. Then an increase to the grain growers of £8 a tonne or so in 1968 heralded the premature death of our large hatching egg exporting business.

From 1968 to '71, I reared poultry commercially at Greenhills and learned the hard edge of commerce. But I also developed a practical knowledge, to add to my professional veterinary knowledge. Looking after the business kept me away from home a lot as I travelled all over the country. I had to leave Lynne alone with Andrew and Sharon about three days a week. She, of course, had no family in Ireland and, apart from the MacHales and Hipwells, very few friends. My aunt Mai and cousin Margaret were extremely supportive and we managed to hang on in there. My farming activities at the time were conducive neither to family harmony nor financial security. I was naive in those days and I got taken to the cleaners on a few expensive occasions. I was getting on Lynne's nerves so much in early 1969 that she dispatched me to the Dew Drop Inn in Kill to have a few pints. It was then that I discovered Guinness for myself and a whole new section of humanity that I never knew existed. It also changed my shape, probably for good and all. I'm trying to change it back.

At the prompting of my friend and veterinary colleague Desmond Mills, I established Greenhills Veterinary Laboratory as a consultancy veterinary practice specialising in the field of intensive livestock production and positive health. Des Douglas of Beecham's was my first client and that started an avalanche of clients and a hyperactive vet consultancy career for the next twelve years.

Des Mills joined me in September of that year and we worked together for about three years until we developed our own specialisation and carried on our practices from our homes. This did not signify a break-up in friendship — far from it.

Lynne became pregnant in that year too with the excitement of it all and our little Ami Jo (Amanda Joanne) was born in the spring of 1972 to rapturous applause. Whereas Andrew and Sharon had been noisy little buggers, Amanda was sweetness, peace and quiet itself — a charming child, the spitting image of her father in looks and temperament.

My speciality practice built up very well. Lynne had learned to type and to keep accounts and we prospered in a small way. However, we had incurred liabilities from farming that were crippling to pay off. I had committed large amounts of borrowed money to housing and equipment which would normally have taken me about ten years to repay. Then Dad had to sell the farm in 1972, a hard blow for us all. The acquisition of the house on the carriageway and its resale to Jonathan Irwin of Goff's helped to ease the burden temporarily but then we had to build another home. Jonathan was and is a good man: he gave us a year to become properly organised before we had to vacate our first family home.

Despite our many, many good times together as a couple and as a family, I found it increasingly difficult to reach a harmonious level of personal relationship with Lynne. Both of us were stubborn, she more than me, but I was hot-headed and voluble.

We disagreed and fought a lot and this hindered the natural development of a mature married relationship. This is relatively easy to reflect on in hindsight but it was very difficult at the time.

Three children, a husband and frustrated, retired rugby player, the remnants of a not very successful farming enterprise and a developing full-time vet practice and business took up an inordinate amount of Lynne's daily life. I was working extremely hard over long hours, often travelling 350–400 miles a day for five days a week. At the end of each day we were both exhausted and didn't have the knowledge or the sense to make 'quality' time for each other. Additionally, Lynne suffered from post-natal depression after Amanda was born and was living on tranquillisers for a time. I remember booking a quick holiday in Majorca and throwing all those damned tablets out of the window as we sped up the dual carriageway towards the airport. About one dozen large Bacardis and Coke later we landed in Majorca and the tablets were forgotten and have been since, thank God.

We enjoyed that holiday — as well as others in West Cork and Kerry — but only in the sense of physical relaxation. On a more intimate level, Lynne and I were not developing any deeper bonds. I really loved her hugely but her feelings for me were more restrained — almost sisterly. This drove me spare, because I was (and am) only flesh and blood — with the emphasis on flesh. I was frustrated naturally.

I knew that she had regretted getting married so young and I understood this feeling. Twenty years of age is far, far too young. She really didn't know men at all and had never developed the sexual maturity that all young women should experience before they settle down.

I knew that she half-resented me as a consequence. I was not able to cope with that and was left with an unanswered question hanging like a worn-out fly paper: 'What the hell can I do about it now? We're married and cannot turn the clock back eight years.'

What we did — on Lynne's initiative — was to get out of ourselves. We both joined the Co. Kildare Tennis Club in Naas and probably for the first time since she arrived in Ireland in 1967 she felt her life had a proper social dimension. There she met a host of new friends — the Hayes, O'Sullivans, Greelys, Barretts, Conways, Lyons, O'Neills and so on. It was a new lease of life for both of us and especially for Lynne. It seems such a simple thing to have done, in retrospect, but it made a big difference at the time.

In 1973–4 I began to play rugby again thanks to my old friend Dave O'Leary's perspicacity and tenacity. This was to change my life irrevocably. I rejoined Blackrock College RFC and began to enjoy non-pressure rugby, while Lynne joined the ladies' committee of Rosa Kelly, Vonnie McLoughlin, Deirdre Costello, Mary Brophy and all the others. This brought us much closer because we began to share good times together. I captained Rock in 1974–5: we won the Leinster Senior League and, apart from the Senior Cup, every other competition and trophy in Leinster as well.

The redoubtable Dan McCarthy was club president and Tom Cleary, late of Wanderers and early of Flogas, was coach — or as Ray McLoughlin said: 'The only guy in the club who can tell Mick Doyle what to do.' But there was method in my madness. In 1975, I coached or tried to coach Fergus Slattery's Rock team. Under Slats' expert advice I sold our house to Goff's Bloodstock Agency and Lynne and I designed and built our dream house — a Guildway-built home to our own specification at Barr-na-Coille, a beautifully secluded idyllic, wooded 1½ acre mature site behind Johnstown village high above Naas — the house that we had both talked about all those years ago during the balmy courting days in Somerset and Kerry.

Around this time John Greely had talked me into chairmanship of the tennis club and there followed three years of great fun and comradeship. With Barrett, Barry O'Sullivan, Charlie Hayes and a few others we formed the all action Naas 7th team. We represented the club at everything except tennis — drinking, joking, wenching (in thought only) and travelling, in fact anything with an -ing in it.

In our new home, we made a new life for our three children, two dogs and four kittens. Barr-na-Coille was and still is one of the most beautiful sites I have ever seen. Lynne and I developed shrubs and flowerbeds, lawns and hedges. We pruned apple trees and grafted new varieties to old stock, an unbelievably satisfying thing to do, especially when you see the results of your labours in the spring.

We spread 220 tonnes of top soil to create sloping lawns and trucked 30 tonnes of beautiful quartzite stone from Glenealy, Co. Wicklow. Paddy Burke from Kilcullen created all the borders and miniature walls from this old stone.

It all developed into a beautiful, secluded, sheltered haven and I adored it there. Our immediate next-door-through-the-hedge neighbours were Antonia and Tim Wardell and their family — Anthony, David, Mike and Henrietta. Tim was a superb photographer, great guitar player, passable BMW motor bike rider, great raconteur and an easy companion. Antonia was a charmer, full of life and zest — and beautiful with it. We all got on like old pals and spent many a boozy, long night talking and dreaming under the stars on the patios or around great log fires drinking mulled wine and generally talking rubbish.

Antonia and myself took up jogging together — the vertical type, thank you very much — and that was the germ of the idea for a TV appearance together. When I took up coaching Leinster in 1978 Antonia was involved in the making of the RTE programme *Positively Healthy*. Over a few pints in Martin Nolan's pub in Kilteel we agreed that she and I would do a programme on jogging — how to begin, the medical check-up, the shoes, the gear etc. It was to be aimed at people who were being encouraged to get fit and stay healthy. We were to meet in Herbert Park in Ballsbridge at 2.15 p.m. one Wednesday early in May, fit and ready to run.

Unfortunately it coincided with Spring Show week and I found myself having to break out of a large lunch in the Hibernian Hotel where the red wine, gin and port flowed freely. Jogging was the farthest activity from my conscious mind at 2.00 p.m. Having changed in the corridor of a nearby bakery I arrived ready for action and falling over myself with enthusiasm. I was full of food and mellow from the effects of the grape. As the weather was changing from bright to dark the unfortunate producer had to wait for some sort of constant light to facilitate filming so he fed us brandy to keep us warm.

The film crew were organising their equipment and we were keeping ourselves warm. The cameraman had to kneel in an invalid chair facing backwards and balance his camera on the shoulders of the guy who was pushing him! The mate, a Corkman, was to run along with the wheelchair on the strip of tarmac that crosses the park while we were to jog alongside on the grass with Antonia asking me all the right questions.

I was supposed to have been the jogging expert. But a bellyful of prime roast beef and a good claret is a pretty lousy preparation for loping along with an extremely attractive companion or, indeed, anybody else.

Anyway, the weather accommodated us and off we trotted with the cameraman being pushed along by this Corkman about two yards ahead of us. It was fine for the first couple of takes but as the afternoon wore on the wine began to bathe the 'jogging centres' in the brain and naturally I began to slow up. Antonia, running beside me, was in danger of becoming passively drunk with all the alcohol fumes wafting her way everytime I answered one of her questions. To make matters worse the Cork wheelchair pusher had found his second wind and started to show off. He acted as if he was in an All-Ireland wheelchair-pushing competition and was even clicking his heels in the air with every second stride. It was all right for him, he didn't have to talk as well. Anyway, I couldn't keep up with him and had to tell him to slow down and stop acting the bollox.

We finally got that part of it finished and took a well-earned breather. As the weather was about to change again, we had to do some more rapid takes with Antonia and myself running around the camera and the extended 'mike' in a circle, while I had to suck in my wayward gut, smile, pick up my steps and display how a runner should develop his or her own style and cadence. At the same time, I was talking and trying to stop Spotty, Antonia's Jack Russell, from choking himself on my laces. Eventually and mercifully we got all the filming done before the weather deteriorated further and I think we adjourned somewhere to warm up. The whole thing was incredible fun and totally unreal. That particular episode in the programme looked great. In fact both of us looked the part on the TV screen. And they tell you that the camera doesn't lie? Ask Joan Collins!

We were all happy at Barr-na-Coille in a warm, lazy sort of way. David was mad on horses, Andrew Doyle and Hennie Wardell had discovered kissing and Amanda, Sharon and Emily Power Smith were spying on them. We had endless, beautifully simple barbecues in summer. Also we held three tennis club barbecues at Barr-na-Coille which are never to be forgotten: tents, pubs, music, super steaks from Johnny Lawless in Kill and everyone committing mental adultery. Happy days indeed.

We were shattered when Antonia and Tim split up and the family moved away. Thankfully we have kept contact and can renew fleetingly those halcyon days of Barr-na-Coille and Garry Ard. Little did I know that it was to be a portent of what would befall us a few short years later.

I was elected a Leinster sub-selector in 1978 together with Ian Cairnduff, Maureen's better half. Then the following year the Leinster Selectors chose me as coach and I enjoyed those five amazing years of which you'll be hearing more any chapter now.

Coaching at that level and my veterinary and business career were more than a full-time occupation. Things began to unravel again between Lynne and myself, despite our more relaxed surroundings. I found it totally impossible to understand her at that time. I had done everything possible to make and develop a home for her and the kids; I was working assiduously at my practice and business but it didn't seem to matter. It seemed to me to be accepted as par for the course but not part of an on-going, developing, maturing relationship.

I couldn't comprehend for example when I came home in the evenings why I didn't receive any kind of warm welcome — like a kiss and a cuddle and a 'how are ye, Mick'.

I wondered at times if I was a big, soft, stupid fool alight with sentimentality. But I know now I wasn't. There was obviously a huge void that I could not fill no matter what I did. Lynne and myself tried to talk about it but we merely skirted the subject.

Perhaps Lynne was pushing me to make my discovery, realise that there was no future for us and make the first move. If she was, I must have been too thick or too self-centred to see it.

I am an impulsive person by nature and a born optimist. Lynne by comparison is more of a pessimist — a realist if you will. She certainly saw the realities of our marriage sooner and was trying to tell me but I was obviously building a cotton wool wall around myself. I know I was bewildered and angry and afraid or unable to contemplate the inevitable. The mental obstacle was looming larger and larger and there seemed to be nothing I could do about it. I suppose it is quite a familiar scenario but it was incomprehensible to me then.

As things began to reach crisis point I knew that Lynne had stopped even pretending that she fancied me physically. I was shattered. She even told me that if I wished to go out with another girl she would understand. I didn't wish. I wanted my own woman. Lynne and I tried to discuss things together but obviously continued to skirt the issues or the main problem. She was too nice to spell it out: I was too afraid to face up to it.

In sixteen years of marriage I had had two fruitless flings and one very good relationship with a warm, loving woman called Julie, to whom I owe a bigger debt than I can ever repay. She kept me sane. We consulted a caring Dominican priest who eventually told us that we were incompatible and then we knew our marriage was going through the death throes. Here we were, two normal people who liked and respected each other very much, with three great kids, a lovely home and a good business — high profile people with everything seemingly going our way and we were a failure and about to break up. Marriage guidance counselling? We should have had it in 1966, sixteen years earlier!

The split-up was precipitated with headlong speed by the fact that both Lynne and I had inevitably met new partners almost simultaneously and had fallen for them . . . Bill and Maria respectively.

We went away on separate holidays with our 'new friends' but in my case it was a disaster. I kept on missing the kids and couldn't wait to get home. I simply did not want to end our marriage.

It was when I was away with the Leinster team in Biarritz that Lynne phoned to tell me that my Auntie Mai had died. We were both heartbroken. Both of us loved her enormously; she had helped to keep us together all the days of our married life and did much more for us besides. She had raised me from birth and was my 'surrogate' mother. Now she was gone. As Lynne said to me in our kitchen in Barr-na-Coille, 'Mick, nothing will ever be the same again.' And it certainly was not.

We got in touch with Brian McLoughlin — a friend to both of us and now the Leinster coach, and asked him to help us to separate legally. He would act for both of us, not one side. We sat down over a bottle of vodka and wrote out our own separation agreement. No arguments but joint free decisions. This was the key to our future altered relationship based on mutual respect and trust.

My Dad had heard about our situation and flew back from holidays in Spain to talk to us. He told us he loved us both, asked us if we were both intent on separating and if we had reached an agreement. We answered affirmatively. He then said, 'I will not take sides and will respect both of your wishes.'

'Micheál', he said, 'you will have to be man enough to allow Lynne to have any man she likes as her friend and to stay with her in the house. She has to have the same rights and freedoms that you will have.'

Of course that was agreed. He told me that I must be prepared to look after her and the kids at all times and at all cost and to support Lynne in public and in private. When you love somebody, as I did, that is easy. Dad's timely intervention was of enormous help. So too was Ray McLoughlin's — probably my oldest friend together with Ned Thornton. Another mutual friend, Andy Butler, sorted out our financial matters.

Ray phoned me at the time of our separation and asked how I was. Without waiting for an answer he said 'I'll give you the same advice you'd give me. Put the children first, Lynne second and yourself last in that order and you'll be doing the right thing.' I confirmed that I had arrived at that decision already. He asked me if I minded Lynne's alliance with Billy. I replied that I didn't. 'Suppose Doyler that it did annoy you. What would you do about it,' he asked.

I answered that I would break his bloody face. (I hoped I was speaking metaphorically). Ray said laughingly, 'You're okay then, I've no worries about you.'

Ned Thornton also helped in his own inimitable way and I am beholden to both of them.

How to tell the children that we were separating legally for keeps was awfully hard — certainly the most painful thing I have ever had to do. We agreed that I would tell Andrew and Lynne would explain to the girls, Sharon and Amanda.

I took Andrew to the West with me for a drive on vet farm calls and explained as best I could how Mum and I were not hitting it off for quite a long time and that we would be better off living apart. We would continue working together and we would be jointly responsible for the love and care of the three of them. We were both in bits when we returned from Mayo. Lynne and the girls were in the same condition at home. Having moved out my personal belongings to a rented house in Naas I remember walking around the orchard and the lawns of Barr-na-Coille, Toberton, Johnstown, Naas with the two dogs, Sarah and Toby, for the last time.

Nothing but good times raced through my mind's video in incredible colour — from the very first day in Bristol long ago when I met her and fell totally in love with her — right up to the present awful times when, still loving her, I was leaving our home and our life together forever: and I didn't want to. It was as if I was on a carousel.

I sat on the apple tree branch and cried and cried and cried. I can still feel it ten years later as if it were now.

I think it was the worst time of my whole life, the pain of loss, futility, defeat and failure all jumbled together, mocking past mistakes and promising only an empty future.

7

Coaching Leinster

'I knew what I wanted, and they knew what I wanted; I knew what they wanted and pretty soon the Leinster players knew what they wanted themselves.' (MESELF 1979)

I TOOK over managing Leinster when Kevin Flynn resigned the job to concentrate on being an Irish selector. So I owe Flynner quite a lot.

Leinster, as in previous years, had very good players but the best players were not always selected. They rightly concentrated on their own rugby career prospects and neglected the cause of their province. Few would blame them. On the night of my appointment I asked Roly Meates, the celebrated fast-food merchant(!) and dentist, who had coached Leinster aeons earlier, if he had any one specific piece of advice for me. He said 'Doyler, you'll go nowhere with these guys unless you can get them to play for something.' I said, 'Thanks Roly, I'll get them to play for Leinster.'

The selection committee of Michael Cuddy (The Cud) as Chairman, Paddy Madigan (The Happy Hooker), Kevin Flynn, Roly Meates and Brian Cross had selected me. Flynner expressed the opinion that I might not have the time to coach Leinster. I replied that if I hadn't then I wouldn't be here! But he had a point. Roly voiced his serious concern that I was at a major disadvantage — I had not attended courses or come through the 'coaching system', whatever that was. I pointed out that I had captained most teams I played with or at least led the forwards. I explained that at

71

Leinster and higher representative levels what the players required was not coaching but rather man management, goal setting, motivation and encouragement. I am utterly unshakeable in that belief, and I am perfectly happy that I never attended a coaching course — or at least the courses that have prevailed then or since.

We all repaired to Milltown Golf Club, having picked a squad of 46 players and enjoyed a raucous dinner. Chairman Cuddy and I met frequently over the summer and discussed the task in hand. We identified the needs of the moment: honest professional selection, respect for players and their well-being, meaningful squad training sessions and the urgency above all of developing quickly into a club side to which players would give their allegiance and whose play would properly reflect the enormous talent that was always available in Leinster but which had been squandered or neglected and frequently abandoned at the altar of coaching.

Added to this of course was that magic elusive ingredient — fun! We agreed that the 'special case' of Willie Duggan would be properly handled and that there would be no ridiculous demands about travelling from Kilkenny to every training session. Here was a man who was self-employed in the industrial electrical contract services field; he had responsibility for major contracts and couldn't afford the luxury of free time or travel. Willie had forgotten more about rugby than most players and selectors I knew had ever learned. Cud and I were adamant that we would accommodate him. I'm glad we did — so were the players.

As the season's start approached I sought the views of the senior pros — Slatts, Willie, Philly Orr, Johnny Moloney, Ollie Campbell and Freddy McLennon. Their advice was succinct, practical, relevant and most welcome. Without it I could not have functioned as I did.

Cud and I simplified our roles. Cud was to 'bring' the selectors 'to' the players and I would give the players confidence in their selectors. In this way we built an honest, stable, happy family. My role was basically to decide on the type of game Leinster would develop, and all the strategies and tactics we could employ. I had to identify and explore each player's potential and utilise it as fully as possible: proper training routines needed articulation and decision. This evolved as we went along. Everyone's view was sought and listened to.

At our first training session in Donnybrook in August 43 players turned up. Cud opened proceedings in his own inimitable style — he thanked the lads for coming and offered them a new future. I thanked Flynner for retiring from coaching and giving me the opportunity to manage Leinster! I promised exciting, total rugby and meant it; I promised fair treatment for everyone, the abolition of the Sacred Cow Syndrome (Slatts laughed at that) and I demanded that everyone had to look after their own fitness. I also extracted from that group of players — a superb mixture of youth and experience — the vow that we would cut out all the crap and shame of yesteryear and put Leinster in its rightful place at the top. I wanted them to have the right to dream their dreams and I was making them responsible for their own destiny. I was merely their guide.

How they took up the challenge and responded is now history but the history books cannot tell from mere statistics the dedicated pursuit of excellence, the sacrifices and disappointments, the striving for harmony or the creation of one of the most wonderful extended teams — players, selectors and alickadoes — that I have ever encountered. The emphasis changed from 'the Leinster team' to 'Leinster', a subtle change of title but a monumental change in commitment.

Looking back on those five fabulous years I can remember even the smallest details. My overall feelings are those of enormous personal gratitude to the players and the gratification of success in all its aspects. I think happily of the pride, the enduring comradeship that prevails and the incredible fun that I know few teams ever experience.

The record of Leinster in that period is available for anyone who bothers to look it up. I would, however, like to record some of the memorable occurrences and thankfully not all of them refer to rugby itself. My first assignment with Leinster was to play the Cheshire XV in Douglas to celebrate the Manx parliament millennium or something.

Paddy Conroy (now sadly deceased), affectionately known as 'Friar Tuck', was in charge of ensuring that all the planning and arrangements worked like clockwork. Having established what I wanted he headed for the Isle of Man on the first plane with an advance party including Van Esbeck, Diffley and Johnston — the media mafia. The team and selectors travelled later and arrived about 10 minutes behind schedule. An exhausted and worried Friar Tuck met us and unfolded a litany of woes — no team room, no dinner (too late), no late breakfast, didn't know the ref's name, time of the match or our estimated time of departure from the hotel to the grounds — the usual itinerary details; he hadn't met the Isle of Man Rugby Committee either. However, says Friar, Masses are every hour on the half hour — 9.30, 10.30, 11.30 etc.

Having arranged things as well as possible we headed for 10.30 Mass on Sunday morning to find ourselves at the tail-end of the previous one with the next Mass beginning at 11.00 a.m. The Cud was beside himself, and me as well, and cried out in his characteristic 'small boy' voice with umbraged expression — 'Jaysus, the bollox even got the times of Mass wrong.' The congregation couldn't understand how thirty or so grown men could laugh so much during a religious ceremony.

Later that night at the dinner and post match atrocities in a superb nightclub everyone was in good form. A comedian whose opening (and closing) three minutes was solely concerned with unfunny anti-Irish jokes collected a few ice cubes on his forehead and fled the stage judiciously. I was physically removed from my table and put up on the stage to fill in for him. He wasn't a hard act to follow and I survived. The singer, Miss something or other, was a brilliant entertainer and was a great hit for the lads — she came back on stage and did a few extra numbers with a well-known English exile, Piggy Powell of Northampton. We won the match as well. Ollie Campbell captained the side and nobody played very well. However it was a start and we came home happy.

Our first home game was against Connacht in Dublin — coached and motivated well by Mick Heaslip, Danno's brother. We invented a short penalty option called 'Heaslip' in Cud's honour. He had issued dire warnings of what would befall the team if we allowed Connacht to beat us: what would be even worse he said would be the thought of those Heaslips swanning around on Saturday night taunting us. We were very lucky to scrape home in the end with a score inspired by Rodney O'Donnell and Joe Brady. That didn't keep the Heaslips quiet but Cud and the rest of us were happy: our team had leapt the first hurdle.

We beat Llanelli well a few weeks later in Lansdowne Road. Fergus Slattery couldn't play but was well substituted for by young Niall Gaffney of Clontarf. However I had no pack leader now so I phoned Willie Duggan at his home at 7.30 on the morning of the game and asked him to do the honours. He told me to piss off with myself and put the phone down. He then rang back two minutes later and said, 'Doyler, I'll do it for you on two conditions. First of all' he said, 'I want the Christian names of all the forwards and their positions and secondly I want you to let me talk in my own way to the backs at the team talk.' I agreed, naturally, but inquired as to why he needed the Christian names and positions of the Llanelli forwards. He told me he knew them and that it was the Leinster forwards he didn't know! He had a brilliant match against his old mate and adversary Derek

Quinnell — another great man.

We beat Ulster next in Dublin in an uneventful sort of game:they had a promising team but we were a bit better organised and just about deserved to win.

We had selected John Robbie as captain for the Llanelli game. The old pros on the team concurred. We deliberately didn't have him captain earlier because it was not opportune for many reasons — for one, he wasn't hail fellow well met with the lads, who didn't really know him. Secondly, he was foolish enough to ask for an 'audience' with Cuddy and myself at the training session following his nomination and demanded to know why he wasn't consulted beforehand. The answers he got left him under no doubt whatsoever who was in charge and responsible for Leinster rugby, the well-being and development of the players and the team. He accepted of course and we were happy we had made the correct decision and had a captain with spunk, abrasiveness and a fair measure of arrogance. We all knew where we stood. He was generally an excellent captain and Leinster did well under him, until he went off to South Africa to seek fame and fortune.

Munster was the final hurdle in our first year and in Thomond Park too — the graveyard of many a visiting team's dreams. The battle lines were drawn — Ollie had replaced Wardie as Ireland's outhalf in Australia the previous summer and Pa Whelan lost his test place to Ciaran Fitzgerald. Ideas of what Munster were going to do to Leinster abounded for weeks before the game. However we won playing 'Munster' rugby by that handsome margin 4–3.

We next played the Italian national team coached by Pierre Villepreux in Donnybrook on a Sunday after Christmas. We were to have a training spin in College Park on Saturday afternoon — we had it all right, but without Willie Duggan. I later found him installing some electrical gear in a remote Kilkenny Design store somewhere around the back of Trinity

College! I sat on a box and talked to him and shared a few fags while he worked. We discussed the match and our strategy, had a few pints and went home. He played a proverbial blinder the following day. He always did and the other players responded mentally and physically to him. It was only shortsighted selectors who couldn't accommodate him — he didn't fit the preconceived mould. I'm glad he didn't and I respected him for his choice of priorities — most of the time.

Before that Italian game Philly Orr asked me in the dressing room if I would indicate to him from the bench when there was only three minutes to full time. I was still puzzled until I indicated four minutes left to play. He dived to the ground, rolled around in agony and was carried off by a solicitous Joe Doran. Hey presto! On comes Mick Jackman — Philly's old Wesley front row partner — with the sweat pouring off him! He had obviously been 'warming up' in urgent anticipation of Philly's sudden injury! Jackman got his first Leinster cap and no-one deserved it better. Mick was a great member of the 'expanded' Leinster team and we were delighted for him and proud of Philly Orr's thoughtfulness.

Victor Brophy, from the bench, announced that 'the last three minutes of Jackman magic has been brought to you courtesy of Old Wesley and Phil Orr'. Paddy O'Brien, our doc, asked Philly as he was being led to the dressing room and the 'casualty area' of a warm shower — 'Nothing trivial I hope Philip?' We beat the Italians well and played our best rugby of the season. We were developing into a formidable force still exploring its potential and we had a brilliant group of players.

We had accepted a summer tour to Romania and were eager to prepare for it towards the end of the Leinster cup campaign. Some players were still engaged in opposing sections of the competition and would be meeting in the semi-finals and the final. Consequently it was difficult to get full attention at training — it was all a bit unreal. I asked Cud for advice and he said he would give the players a piece of his mind. He arrived early to Donnybrook for the squad session and could be seen pensively pacing the Bective Rangers' dance floor working himself up into a frenzy. When all the lads were installed in the dressing room The Cud burst in through the door purposefully and straight away stepped into the rubbish bin: there was an immediate silence at Cud's signal and he said; 'Lads, I've something to say to yez, your whole attitude to training is wrong and the whole scene is far too fucking washy-wishy [*sic*] for me!' The whole room erupted: even The Cud himself couldn't suppress his laughter but everyone got the message and got down to the task at hand.

We had to get extra sponsorship to undertake the trip to Romania — presents for our hosts and funds to take Slatts with us for the first game together with a replacement for him when he returned home. Luckily, some good friends of mine contributed to our funds — namely Bobby Barden (Old Wesley and Saab), Eddie Barr and Eddie O'Meara (from Peugeot) and Ray McLoughlin (from himself). Tom Keaveney of Gilbeys donated a cartload of Baileys Irish Cream Liqueur, Irish Distillers contributed Paddy whiskey and Guinness threw in engraved mugs, bottle openers and such like. Puma supplied the gear for which we were grateful.

We brought a youthful Paul Dean instead of Seamus Oliver Campbell who had gone to South Africa with the Lions and Dessie Fitzgerald, a Trinity yuppie from the Roly Meates School of Propping. Both contributed handsomely and fitted into the team like old hands.

It was a memorable trip. We stayed overnight in a hotel near London Heathrow on the outward journey. It was the first and last time I ever slept in a room with Michael Cuddy. He snored like an out-of-tune lawnmower; he mowed every blade of grass around Heathrow that night stopping now and then to fill up with petrol, check the oil and empty the grass collector. Frank Kelly once referred to Larry Cunningham as the only subterranean singer in the world and felt that it would normally take two men to sing as low as Larry. Cud was like that.

We made a mess of the first game. J.R. (Robbie) took some crazy options, to our disgust in the dug-out and to that of Slatts who was pack leader. For the next match in Constanţa I curtailed Robbie's authority and took over the team. In Slatt's absence we made Mick Jackman pack leader. He was brilliant: we won the match and Paul Dean at outhalf heralded his enormous talent with one of the finest tries I *ever* saw. That was the first match I had ever seen him play and he left an indelible impression on me.

We had a grand bunch of travelling alickadoes — Paddy (The Bulge) Bolger, Victor and Niall Brophy, Collie Smith, and John Joe White. David Walsh (*Irish Press*), Kieran Rooney (*Irish Independent*) and Derek Jones (*The Irish Times*) made up the press corps. Every night we met for a nightcap or six in Manager Cuddy's room and often had to be driven to bed by the players.

After the game in Constanţa we attended a superb dinner hosted by the Romanian Minister for Sport and Tourism. Cud and Victor Brophy got him pissed with a combination of Paddy whiskey and Bailey's Irish Cream. I was asked by The Bulge to 'wind him up' — so I did. I asked him, for example, what he found wrong with capitalism. He declared that it was the exploitation of the masses by the few. I said that this sounded more like communism. Fuming, he asked me how I could say that, to which I replied: 'Minister, why are all the players in one room by themselves having a crap dinner while you have summoned us in here to a private room to have a superb dinner with you?' The Cud broke into *McNamara's Band* to divert his attention, but he was raging. The situation was saved when our players, led by Mike Gibson (not *the* Mike Gibson), broke into this private room and made Cud and myself join them on our knees walking around singing the Dwarfs' Chorus. 'High-ho High-ho!' The minister's entourage were nonplussed by this outbreak of democracy.

Our last night in Romania was hilarious. We had attended the Romania v. Russia game. Most of Russia's best players were reported to be in Afghanistan. Every time a Romanian scored he came back and bowed to the Minister of Sport! The 'Rat' Kennedy cheered in his lonely little boy soprano voice for Russia — but in vain. After dinner we left our players in the company of their Romanian and Russian counterparts and the rest of us paid the Bucharest Hilton a visit. At that time it was a beautiful place, but an insult amid the squalor that the poor people of Bucharest were forced to accept from Ceaucescu and his stooges. We found on our return all three teams carousing with abandon and wearing each other's gear. Someone stole or misappropriated Cud's last bottle of Paddy which was to have been our parting nightcap. He stood desolately in the middle of his room observing to his parched fellow-travellers, 'That's not fair gentlemen. The manager's room is sacrosect (sic).' We all knew what he meant.

When Cud came down to breakfast the following morning the room was full of players but absolutely deafening silence reigned. Cud and the players were keeping their distance. I introduced three Russian 'heavies' to Cud and told him that they wanted Leinster to tour Russia next year! He looked up from his novel and the remnants of a ravaged black pudding and said quietly but firmly; 'Would yez fuck off back to Russia and get out of Afghanistan.' The players roared their approval, the Russians shagged off and The Cud beamed. The balance had been restored and we came home happy.

It had been a memorable first season and we looked forward to the next few exciting years. There was one piece of bad news awaiting us, however. Rodney O'Donnell had received a serious, almost catastrophic, neck injury in South Africa with the Lions during the summer which put an early end to an enormously promising career.

In the closed season, an unprecedented social event took place. The Leinster selectors and their ladies threw a dinner for the Leinster players and their ladies! Simple, but no-one had ever thought of it before. It was an important occasion as well as an enjoyable one. We had established a bond of respect and trust between selectors and players. We all now talked of 'us', no longer of 'us and them'. Selectors no longer needed to mention players from their own clubs for selection because our system ensured fair play, fair selection and looking after the best interest of all the players and of Leinster. To their credit, the clubs accommodated us as best they could and it all added up to a golden era of Leinster rugby. We had set ourselves patterns and targets and levels of achievement and performance that served as our benchmark for the next four seasons.

We had the most incredible fun as well. We won an historic three interprovincial championships in a row (later to be eclipsed by a superb Ulster squad who followed our example). In five years we won four championships outright and shared one with Munster; Munster drew once with us and beat us once in Dublin. One game against Munster changed me irrevocably. We won 18–9 or something like that — six penalties from Ollie Campbell. Afterwards, I met Tom Cleary — a good friend who knew me well — outside the Wanderers' pavilion. He looked me straight in the eye and said, 'Mick if you accept today's win and the rugby Leinster played as par for the course you'll be letting down a lot of people, yourself included. You can do a lot better than that.' He was right. I went home sober and early that night.

I met the team in Donnybrook the following Wednesday and challenged them to score 50 points against Ulster in Ravenhill the following Saturday week! We won 39–9 and missed about three more tries. That was some performance. It was also the best team of footballers that I have ever coached. For the record I'll name them : Hugo MacNeill,

Freddy McLennon, Paul McNaughton, Ian Burns, Frank Quinn, Ollie Campbell, John Robbie, Philip Orr, John Cantrell, Mick Fitzpatrick, George Wallace, Gerry Holland, Ronan Kearney, Willie Duggan and Fergus Slattery. John Robbie retired twenty minutes from full time with a feigned injury to give Palmerston's great scrum half Barry O'Connor his first Leinster cap.

Ulster were stunned but gracious about our victory: we were ecstatic. At the dinner in Bangor Jim Donaldson, an Ulster selector, turned to Ned Thornton and said 'Well now Eddie, what do you think of Ulster rugby after that little debacle this afternoon?' Ned, never short of a remark, said, 'Do you know that white flag yez have with the red hand on it?' 'Aye', said Jim, 'The Ulster flag.' 'Well', said Ned, 'I'd take the red hand off it and surrender if I were you!'

The following year, at the return fixture in Dublin, the new Ulster coach, Willie John McBride, asked me if I could arrange for Joe Doran to bring out the oranges to the Ulster team at half-time as he, Willie John wanted to sit in the stand. I said fine, that I'd do the Leinster team and let Joe do Ulster. That night at the dinner Roy Lockheed, the Ulster president, was joking about the way I brought out the oranges to Leinster at half-time. At this, Ned Thornton scribbled a hasty note to John Robbie who was next to speak. Robbie read out the note, which said: 'Mick Doyle would not have had to go near the Leinster team at half-time had Ulster brought down their own orangeman!' This naturally brought the house down.

After our first year, with the selectors' approval and the nod from the senior players, I had brought Ned in to help me look after the players properly. He was invaluable and made a big contribution to the development of the team. His wit was matched by his astuteness. As Flynner, Paddy Madigan and Brian Cross departed, equally good people joined our selectorial board, Vinnie McGovern, Ken Ging, Colm Smith, Eddie Coleman, Eric Campbell and Tony Twomey. Eddie Coleman succeeded The Cud as chairman in my fifth year.

We travelled within Ireland by train to the away games and those train journeys on Friday afternoons were hilarious. The Leinster Under-20 team always accompanied us with their selectors and handlers. We used to occupy the small bar area and drink until our destination — we spilled most of it.

The hospitality in Belfast, Galway, Limerick and Cork was always of the highest order but I must admit that trips to the West were my favourite. Galway had a draw to it that was irresistible. The Galway sports ground-cum dog track is one of the most exposed pitches ever to play rugby on and the rain is something else. It always rained when we played there but still we gave some of our best performances, probably because our control of the ball had to be absolute. Cuddy and myself always 'led the pack' from the far touchline and were able to say nasty things to the referee and touch judge without being overheard by the disciplinary committee. The Cud abused the Leinster backline on one visit and Micky Quinn at outhalf stopped the game and told him to shut up and piss off. The Cud's reply was a classic, but unprintable. Of course there was no rancour.

We entertained Llanelli, South of Scotland, Wellington and Romania in Dublin during the next few years but the IRFU would not let us play a major touring side — probably in case we would win and Ireland wouldn't! After we played Romania in Donnybrook in the 1980–81 season John Reason of the *Daily Telegraph* approached Willie Duggan and myself as we came off the pitch. Willie had just played one of the best games I'd seen him play for Leinster. John asked me for my observations on the game. I replied that we had decided to go out in the first half to soften them up and kick the proverbial shit out of them. Duggan drew deeply on his cigarette butt and through a halo of carcinogens fixed a beady eye on Reason and said: 'And it went so well for us, John, that we had a quick word at half time and decided to kick the shit out of them again in the second half!'

We went on tour to Venice, and St Jean de Luz down near Biarritz. We also visited Llanelli and Bristol but we lost.

Venice brings back a host of memories. When we arrived we discovered that the hotel management had put all the players in double rooms with only one double bed! The Ging and I shared a two-bedded room.

Everyone dumped their duty free booze in our room and it became the bar. We got no sleep for a week. A Leinster party led by President Eddie Egan and Il Cuddio travelled in style by gondola limousine to make a presentation to the Mayor of Venice from the people of Dublin.

The official party duly returned having presented the mayor with a beautiful, engraved crystal vase. Now, the mayor turned out to be a socialist and a painter — not in the Michelangelo mould, he was more into Dulux or Bergers — and he was up a ladder painting the palace when they arrived. He came down at the doorman's summons, accepted the crystalware, bowed thrice to the open-mouthed Paddies, handed the prezzie to the doorman and shagged off back up the ladder. It is not on record what the representatives of the people of Dublin said to Doge the Dauber, probably something with sex and travel very prominent.

We also paid a visit to St Jean de Luz, the home of Gerard Murillo who set up the invitation. But on the morning after we arrived Lynne phoned with news of my Auntie Mai's death. I came home immediately — Paddy Conroy accompanied me by taxi to Biarritz airport from where I flew to Paris and then Dublin.

I was truly shattered by Mai's death. She had meant a lot to me, Lynne and especially my cousin Margaret and brother Tom. She was the one person who kept tabs on all of us, worried about us and kept us in touch with one another and with the family at large. She was an incredible woman. She had brought me up almost from birth until I was about six, when she got married herself to Wills Brosnan. Having lived in Castleisland for a while they went to the US for five or six years but came home to settle down in Cork. Their large apartment there became the focal point of many of our activities and a base away from home for all of us. I was very close to Mai, as was Lynne, who, living here in Ireland away from all her folks in Somerset, loved and trusted Auntie Mai.

I will never forget sitting over coffee in the kitchen at Barr-na-Coille, our home, and talking about Mai before we set off for the funeral in Kerry. Lynne and I were both shattered by her totally unexpected death. Things were falling apart between us at the time. That was when she said to me, 'Mick, nothing will ever be the same again.' She was right. We split up soon afterwards and the whole world changed. With Mai's death any chance that Lynne and I may have had to work things out were stifled and gradually evaporated.

Uncle Wills, Mai's husband, died soon after Mai: he could not live without her. He wanted to die to be with her and his wish was granted. They are buried together at Killeenteerna graveyard near Currow.

Soon after Mai's passing I went to live with Maria. Lynne and I had passed the point of no return. Events overtook us and accelerated the final parting of the ways.

During my term with Leinster even greater tragedy struck The Cud. On a cold frosty morning in January his wife Meda and their two lovely daughters were tragically killed in a Co. Kildare road accident. It was naturally a terrible time for him. We met quite a lot during this time and it was then that I developed the respect, love and admiration that I have had for him ever since.

He handled himself so well and helped his son John to come to terms with their awful loss.

A few weeks before we went to tour Romania he met Helen Buckley, a good friend of Lynne and myself. I had introduced her to Cud. He talked a lot about her during moments of solitude in Romania. They got engaged soon afterwards and are now happily married with a young daughter and son. John Cuddy and Helen, his youthful stepmother, are the best of friends.

In 1983 Ollie Campell contracted a serious, undiagnosed health problem which precipitated the early retirement of one of the greatest players it has been my privilege to meet. John Robbie, Frank Quinn and Freddy McLennon emigrated to South Africa.

We drafted in Mickey Quinn as an old campaigner to steady the backline down. Paul McNaughton went off to the USA on IDA business and Rodney O'Donnell's career was over. However, we had in our squad and coming up from the under-20 level some excellent players — Brendan Mullin, Hugo MacNeill, Johnny Murphy, Derek McGrath, Tony Doyle and John McGready.

Eddie Coleman and myself brought Mick Quinn into the set-up and he took to it like a duck to water. He had a huge influence on the backline and the team and it was due to him that they functioned so well.

I remember against Llanelli in Donnybrook he made two sharp breaks inside his own 22 which Brendan Mullin converted into tries. Mickey kicked the first convert and as he came up to attempt the second he approached the press box and shouted to Ned Van Esbeck. 'There you are Ned, two breaks from Quinnie and two tries: I bet Wardie couldn't do that. And I'll kick this convert as well!' He did and the crowd loved it. It was hilarious.

My time with Leinster had a profoundly positive effect on me. We had some brilliant players and we created a great team and squad. Our training sessions were productive and were great fun. We developed every facet of our game to the highest degree and we utilised all our individual and combined talents. Many players from that era went on to play for Ireland. I am enormously proud of all the people who were involved during that time. I am equally cognisant of what Cud and I set out to do and what we achieved.

For both he and I Leinster was like an extended, enlarged family who made us feel part of them. I also met most of the players from the other provinces and I came to respect, admire and like them. I also knew quite a lot about them as I had been assessing them for years!

When I was elected Irish coach in July 1984 I was naturally honoured and elated but I had, simultaneously, a deep sense of loss and sadness departing from my close involvement with Leinster. However I was leaving them in the good hands of Ned Thornton, Eddie Coleman and the other selectors.

As a Kerryman I am proud to be a Munster man but as a rugby man I am unequivocally a Leinster rugby man and without Leinster I would have achieved very little in rugby.

8

Maria – A Change in Tempo

*'I recall a gipsy woman
Silver spangles in her eyes
Ivory skin against the moonlight
And the taste of love's sweet wine.'*
(DON WILLIAMS, 1970s)

I CAME awake from a post-coital snooze and realised that two women, sporting headgear just like Carmelite nuns were peering in over the wall at us. My companion was sound asleep in the crook of my arm, oblivious to the world. Her soft breathing replaced the earlier passionate gulps of air that had punctuated our recent lovemaking.

We were some sight for two gentle nuns to behold! My wellingtons, wet leggings and trousers were strewn with lustful abandon all over the protesting, creaking heathers while the top half of me was enveloped in the layer of clothing one is required to wear while fishing from a boat on Lough Corrib in May. This was in stark contrast to the naked lower half of me.

My companion's state of dishabille was far more fetching. Her wellies were still on her feet while her jeans had gone walkabout. Her bra hung brazenly from an adjacent foxglove and her blouse was airing on a prickly furze. Her knickers, and mine, were off on a magical mystery tour among the local flora and fauna.

I summoned up my flagging courage, covered my half-mast flagpole with the edge of my waxed jacked (she was lying on the rest of it) and shouted softly in nonchalant salutation, 'Howya nuns?' The intrepid duo ducked their heads and legged it off down the hilly road. My beloved woke up at the sound of me clearing my throat and with the barest glimpse at the departing nuns, sat up in all her glory, but without her finery, and said 'Doyler, I thought we were supposed to be on an island!'

So did I, come to think of it. Our noble boatmen and sometime fishing companions, Douglas, Mills and James had landed us on a supposed island in the Corrib and we had all had lunch in this enchanted spot. Afterwards, our heads light with the scent of wild mint and my delightful fawn all soft and loving and overcome with passion for Michael Gerard, my mates pushed off fishing for an hour or so audibly muttering something about . . . 'love in his eyes and murder in his trousers.' They left me in the arms of an *amoureuse* who, before I could ramble on about the beauty of the place, the all-pervading aroma of burning firewood, and being at peace with nature, softly but purposefully said, 'Doyler, cut out the bullshit: come over here I want you.'

I did as I was told and we christened the Hill of Doon. Some island! And I thought nuns could walk on water. Apart from the Hill of Doon I also christened a nasty bastard of a doctor fly who landed and pierced my left buttock at a critical moment and nearly put me off my stroke. Anyway, it was the Hill of Doon on Lough Corrib in Connemara. I was Mick Doyle and my ravishing maiden was Maria — the woman with whom I shared the next three years and who taught me a lot about myself and a whole heap about women, love, sex and life.

She had a profound influence on me for many reasons and it was by sheer chance, like many things in life, that we met. We were both in a group sharing a table at a dress dance in late 1981.

We met on the dance floor and after a few skirmishes, due to me falling over some little bollox doing a nifty quickstep like a Jack Russell after a rat, we settled down to pointing out the things we liked about each other — and we had only just met.

I was a bit pissed — not drunk but nicely warmed up, amorous, aware and verbose. I had just finished some field research work for Beecham Animal Health and had presented my findings to John Watkins, their then veterinary researcher, that afternoon. Of course we had a celebratory drink. Des and Iris Mills came in during our celebrations to take Lynne and me to the dress dance. We got there quite late, naturally, and your woman Maria was at the table.

She was a very attractive vivacious woman who looked stunning in the greeny/brown velvet low-cut evening dress she was trying to wear. We started dancing together and two things soon became clear to me. First, she wasn't wearing a bra. Second, she was wearing a suspender belt and a skimpy G-string, something that excited me more than I can say, because I have always been extremely partial to those particular accessories. Maria and meself sort of reconnoitred each other's bodily territories during our one hour slow waltz — we slow waltzed to *Satisfaction, The Walls of Limerick*, various rumbas and sambas not to mention jigs and the odd reel.

We eventually broke into some unrecognisable rock 'n roll routine in case anyone had noticed that we fancied one another! In the heat of the moment and with rising excitement coupled with the bravado that the presence of an admiring female develops in one I flung my jacket off almost blinding the lead guitar player/singer who fell backwards and knocked over the drummer; the base guitar player began to laugh and the band (all three of them) stopped playing altogether.

Maria and I slid back to the safety of the table and the amusement of the O'Sullivans, Mills and Maria's husband at the time. He was a nice man and he knew what we were up to. Lynne had her views as well. I came home wearing Maria's expensive coat and she wore my dress jacket, having persuaded the lead guitarist, with smiles, wiles and wiggles to part with it.

It was obvious to all of us that Maria and I had fallen for each other. Both our marriages were on their last legs as we knew but probably weren't ready to admit yet.

We met a few times after Christmas and gradually grew to like one another. An affair began to take shape which, probably like all affairs, was exciting, stimulating and somewhat forbidding because of our family circumstances and commitments. She, like me, had three lovely children. The two families started to meet regularly on a social basis and life was both pleasant and one hell of a strain. My feelings were in terrible turmoil. I had 'fallen in love' with Maria while still loving and respecting Lynne. I really didn't wish our marriage to end; and of course I adored my children who were at a very impressionable, vulnerable age. Maria felt the same about her family.

However, we wanted to keep on seeing each other, so we maintained the status quo. Sounds familiar, doesn't it?

We went off to Lanzarote for a fortnight in April but apart from being great fun some of the time it was generally a disaster for both of us. We were both under extreme mental pressure. I couldn't stop thinking about my kids and I was giving the Bacardi and Coke a bit of a lash. After a fortnight punctuated by rows about nothing and making up regularly we came home under great strain and almost gave each other up.

I remember distinctly telling Lynne in our kitchen over coffee what a disaster it had been. However she was in the first flush of her new relationship with Bill and sadly, any hope of a reconciliation between us had long gone.

Maria and I made things up after a few good heart to hearts and after that our relationship really took off. We found that we were most compatible either in bed or thinking about going to bed! I had always felt that I wasn't at all backward in

the bedding-down-with-women department, but I will admit
freely that Maria taught me things about men and women
and their mutual enjoyment that I had either forgotten or
never learned or which had become rusty with the passing
years of marriage. I was a willing pupil. I often told her that
if I took it seriously I'd be good at it! She it was, I believe,
who invented the G spot. She had them everywhere, even in
her handbag. I believe that during our three years together,
I found most of them.

Most of all, Maria made me slow down and relax and
luxuriate in the sheer joy of sex. She was a lovely, loving,
lovable woman — most of the time. At other times she was
the greatest little bitch I had ever encountered. She could be
completely unreasonable and fly off the handle at a moment's
notice. I often told her that she was like a fishwife whose boat
didn't turn up. She was utterly and totally unpredictable.

I'm not the placid type. I could have throttled her on
many occasions, not that I ever would, of course. Instead, I
sometimes playfully put her over my knee, pulled down her
jeans and pants and spanked her with mock seriousness. The
problem was, of course, that we both enjoyed this and,
naturally enough, one thing leads to another and we would
make up during and after some deliciously acrobatic lovings.

Lynne and I had separated amicably and I moved into a
rented house in Naas — just to preserve my independence
and to provide a base for my children and friends to visit me.
It was a good idea too — many a night after a row with Maria
I would walk out in anger and drive 'home' to Naas seething
with temper and pent-up aggression and frustration. I probably should have stayed on and talked things out with her,
and perhaps playfully 'corrected' her.

Of course Maria was going through a horrendous time
too. She was splitting up from her husband, they were selling
their farm and home and she was in search of a new base for
herself and her children.

Not the ideal time for two short-fused people to be carrying on a relationship. However we battled on. It wasn't all rows and making up — far from it. Even in our early days before we went legitimate, as it were, we had some hilarious happenings.

Once we were using friends Tony and Angie's house as a trysting spot when they were on holidays. We had shared a bottle of wine and a languid sinful bath, and having established ourselves under the duvet in a large bed we lay back in delicious anticipation of the exquisite nerve-tingling pleasures we were about to bestow on each other when that little brat of a Corgi — Gussy — started to bark his fucking head off out on the lawn and wake up the whole neighbourhood. Afraid that the neighbours might investigate we experienced a large dose of *coitus interruptus* (or *amplexus reservatus* in Roman circles) and beat a hasty retreat.

On another occasion we had arrived in mid-afternoon at a hotel in the country and with a few hours to while away we slid into our familiar loving routine. We got so carried away and the walls were so thin in our particular room that we were interrupted continually by members of the hotel staff knocking desperately on our door asking Maria if she was all right. There are certain situations when the nuptial bed is jumping around like a trampoline and it is quite difficult to explain to some anxious eavesdropper that you're fine and that your partner isn't murdering you. The glances we got that week-end from the people in the hotel were a mixture of awe, admiration, envy and disbelief.

I began to spend more and more time at Maria's house during the second year of our relationship. We believed we had something going and we probably had. I liked living with Maria and grew very fond of her three children. This often prompted guilt feelings about my own children and how they might be feeling and I tried to be around them as much as possible.

We had basically settled down as a couple and both our broods seemed to get on together. We took them on a few trips at weekends to the Corrib, to Paddy and Mary Clancy's beautiful bungalow at Oughterard. They enjoyed themselves and we made quite a happy extended family.

This was the bungalow Tony James had introduced us to in the beginning, the base for hardy followers of mayfly fishing in May and August. Gary Hart also found its solitude stimulating when he wished to get away from Donna Rice and the media. Had he brought Donna Rice here in the first place he might be President of the US now!

We went to Oughterard on quite a few occasions and occasionally stayed at Harry and June Hodgsons's beautiful Curryreeva House. We also did some fishing — mainly dapping with the mayfly — and it was Maria who caught the fish, not me. I never caught one bloody sprat in the Corrib. It is a beautiful place — I love it and have incredibly happy yet poignant memories of the many times we spent there — but I had no luck fishing there.

I remember shopping for the breakfast things early one Saturday morning in Oughterard village and meeting Brian 'The Body' O'Halloran reading *The Irish Times* over the bonnet of his two-tone blue metallic designer Mercedes 450 SEL, JCB GT. He had just had a row with his gillie over the mayfly. Having driven down from Dublin in the early hours he inquired of the gillie if he had a plentiful supply of mayflies. Yer man said 'No, I thought you had them'. 'No I don't' said Brian 'they ran out of them in Superquinn in Blackrock at five o'clock Friday evening!'

I don't think The Bod caught many fish either — they know a gringo from Dublin when they see one.

All our boats used to pull into an island at a predetermined time for mid-morning drinks, lunch or afternoon tea. When it was sunny we secured a long rope from our boat to a rock and allowed the boat with Maria aboard to float around gently on the water. She is a sun-worshipper and loved to lie out in the boat, nude except for a butterfly loin-cloth, toasting her nubile torso in the Connacht sun. I preferred a six pack of Smithwicks with the shark hunters or a bottle of Paddy whiskey with Corrib water — a grand mixer.

I was, of course, coaching the Leinster rugby team during this time. I was also an Irish rugby sub-selector. I was running a business, or trying to, and simultaneously endeavouring to perfect the successful techniques of embryo transfer in cattle with a team of veterinary colleagues and a good friend of mine, Pat Tattan. To try to accommodate all that with marriage breakdowns on both sides and to establish a decent relation-ship was extremely difficult but nevertheless worth working for. I thought so anyway.

Maria and I had become an established couple — both on the rugby merry-go-round and socially as well. We were prob-ably trying to settle down to rural domesticated respectability. Of course the usual interfering and know-all busybodies of both sexes became involved in our 'arrangement' for their own nefarious reasons but we weathered most of that, for a time anyway.

Maria had mixed effects on me. On the one hand I grew very protective in a masculine way towards her and her children: I felt great love and strong sexual attraction for her and satisfaction and happiness from being close to her.

On the other hand I was never comfortable with her incredible changes in mood and tempo. I wasn't laid back enough or emotionally secure enough myself for that and it had a detrimental effect on our relationship.

Maria sold her house and farm and I helped her to move into a large rented house near Lucan. Both of us hated the place. I spent less time there because we seemed to be drifting inexorably away from each other. I discovered why much later.

We took both sets of children to Menorca on holidays in July 1983. Lynne and I had taken them there when we were a family and we loved the place. Maria didn't like it and didn't really enjoy the holiday. We began the fortnight with Maria, myself and her two youngest in one apartment and her eldest plus Andrew, Sharon and Amanda in another.

After two days of 'expletives deleted' the Doyles finished up in their own apartment — a portent of things to come. However, I think we each enjoyed the holiday with our own kids at any rate. We went snorkelling and diving from pedal boats and had a ball. We all went out to dinner every night and had a reasonably good time together. That was the last time however that both families fraternised like this.

One amusing incident that my own son Andrew never lets me forget relates to snorkelling and showing off. We strolled down the beach, Andrew and me like two posers, the flippers draped with professional nonchalance from thumbs over our shoulders, leaving in our train a gaggle of admiring children to carry the remaining gear. I ensconced myself in one seat of a pedal boat, Andrew in another and the girls draped around us. We pedalled like mad backwards but couldn't get off the bloody beach — to everyone's amusement. I've rarely been as embarrassed. Served us bloody right. Maria and I both came home with our families and resolved to split up. I moved from Naas to the lovely seclusion of Poulaphouca and Pinewood Lodge — as far from Lucan and Maria as possible.

I missed being near her and loving her but the moment had passed. Against my better judgment, we met occasionally and spent some nights together lovingly. However, that only prolonged the agony.

Maria had met and had a brief affair with some other man during the time that we were involved seriously. She had obviously needed to do that. She wasn't really ready for a mature relationship. She wanted to be my girlfriend but I craved and needed more permanence which she was incapable of giving at that time. We drifted further and further apart spiritually even though we did enjoy each other's company when, for example, we spent international rugby weekends together.

The end of my relationship with Maria upset me emotionally to an enormous degree and caused me the most incredible hurt and pain — far more than I had ever experienced with Lynne. This was nobody's fault, really, but it was soul and confidence-destroying. When I went away with Tom Cleary on holidays to Tenerife in June 1984 I was at the lowest ebb of my life. I never knew before what loneliness really meant — that numb, aching feeling that seeps stealthily through your bones and muscles and into your very being. You feel useless and there is no shape or future to your life. You have a heart and mind and body that seem redundant, yet full to capacity and primed with love, affection and caring, willing to bestow these intense feelings on someone who doesn't even have to reciprocate — someone who would just listen and understand. Socially, you enjoy what you can without ever being able to forget the emptiness that awaits you back at the place you now call home.

Even though Mandy has since washed away all the pain and hurt from me I still remember with vivid clarity every single minute when I was so isolated spiritually. One of Kris Kristofferson's songs expressed it well:

'When no one stood behind you
but your shadow on the floor,
and lonesome was more than a state of mind . . .'

Those few lines tell it all, really. If you've been there you'll know what I mean.

I suspect Maria had an identity crisis too and tried to find herself by meeting other men — looking for Mr Right. By this stage I was definitely monogamous and try as I might to frequent the dens of supposed pleasure on the Leeson Street strip — Menopause Alley — I couldn't do it and stayed away.

I find it difficult to ask a woman out just for the sake of it, and unless I meet the right girl at the time I never get involved. As you've probably gathered Maria did switch me on and we might have made a go of things had we met later on. She was a good companion, lively, witty and full of devilment. She had a sexy, throaty laugh that was infectious. She was an excellent cook and a great homemaker. We were compatible in many ways — socially, intellectually and most definitely sexually. This latter common factor probably prevented us from destroying one another. Anyway, in the end we both realised we were not right for each other. Maria met her Mr Right and I met the girl that I had written away to Santa Claus for, so long ago.

I am glad Maria and I shared part of our lives together. I regret not one single second of it. She taught me an awful lot and helped me make up my mind about many things. She helped me to abandon smoking — that most deadly, creeping, polluting insult ever inflicted on the human race. She gave me a handle on drink even though she often drove me to it! She gave me many good perspectives on myself. I loved her intensely and I'm glad I met her. She also gave me more complexes about myself than I ever thought possible — but later these acted as the spur to sort myself out. I am enormously fond of her now and will be 'till I am no more on this earth. My darling Mandy understands this completely and she knows me — and herself.

Maria turned me into a shameless sex maniac — anyone who could perform in front of holy nuns had to be shameless. I hope they've gotten over the experience and forgiven me. In the end, when reminiscing about my time with Maria I feel that I probably wasn't as good as I wanted to be, but at least I am better than I thought I was! I have gone back to the Corrib a few times in the intervening years but the magic has gone and the music has died.

The Hill of Doon will never be the same again.

9

The Cud and I

'A bird in the hand is worth two of George Bush.'
(MICHAEL CUDDY, CIRCA 1990)

THE first time I ever met him was in a bedroom in Cruise's Hotel, Limerick after the post-match festivities. A combined Oxford/Cambridge team, posing as Wolfhounds, had played a selected Munster team. Michael Cuddy was guesting as prop forward for Munster.

We were all sitting around on beds and chairs chatting and joking when suddenly a guillotine-like hush broke out as the The Cud appeared in the doorway. He wore a pair of demotivated jockey shorts that had to be at least three sizes too small and bursting with unfulfilled promise. He also sported a set of frayed garters that supported two red, cattle-jobber socks. This very personal ensemble was topped off by a patchwork quilt worn toga-fashion, presumably from his own bedroom. His alert, all-seeing, beady eyes looked at no-one and everyone simultaneously, and at the time as well, as he would say himself.

He looked like one of Ghengis Khan's bouncers who had just happened on a group of dastardly infidels about to invade the harem. However, eunuch he certainly was not.

He wandered carefully around the room daintily picking his steps through a labryrinth of legs and bodies and camped in a corner under the wash-hand basin and mercifully fell fast asleep. To an impressionable twenty-year-old with burning aspirations to play for Ireland, the Lions and the World, Cud,

99

even then, had an unhappy knack of creating the wrong impression, allowing one foolishly to underestimate him. I thought to myself 'Christ, he can't be a rugby player, can he?'

Twenty years later, for example, the Romanian team were training in Donnybrook prior to their game with Leinster. A member of Bective rugby club, one Des Broderick, was in the dressing room talking to an American friend when The Cud rushed in the door in a fluster, red in the face, wearing wellies, dirty overcoat and a nondescript hat, all normal Cud-wear. He mumbled incoherently, rushing his words, looking for balls for the training session. Having satisfied himself that they were on the way he thanked yer man and walked out. The American visitor turned to our Bective man and said in awe: 'He speaks good English for a Romanian, doesn't he?'

The next time I came up against him was in 1962 when it took P.J. Dwyer, Malachy Coughlan and myself to 'do a job' on him. He was like a bullock in a scrum — one that had been suckling its mother for about two years and had remained out on grass for another few — unhoused and undomesticated.

One could understand why Fanie Kuhn, the South African prop forward, couldn't handle him in the game with Leinster in the early 60s and had to resort to trying to throttle him in self-defence to avoid a goring. Our Michael was one tough hombre.

Michael Cuddy is a remarkable figure of a man, immensely powerful with a big, big frame. His business empire lies in cattle exporting and some would say the white slave trade, exporting rugby players south of the Liffey. He is a very considerate and gentle man, his twin loves being horse-racing and rugby in no particular order. If the truth were known, he probably owns more legs, ears and arses of race horses than any Irishman in the equine spare parts business and has been a very successful owner and punter.

His hobbies are golf, for which he has the 'black belt' (as

a public danger) and verbally abusing Protestant referees, particularly if they look even remotely like John West. Bective Rangers, the club which Tony O'Reilly claims Cud's father bought him for his 21st birthday, has given him a liking for South African rugby players and an aversion to tennis clubs. He likes his food, his Irish whiskey and the occasional Guinness. He also drinks the odd bottle of wine between drinks.

He has devoted much of his life to rugby in almost every facet and he is now the Junior Vice-President of the Irish Rugby Football Union. He is due to be president in the 1992–3 season — a veritable Cud-in-waiting. I have offered to be his script writer: somehow, I don't think he trusts me with words!

I never really got to know him until he and I became chairman and coach respectively in the Leinster rugby set-up in 1978. We apparently had impressions of each other which were incorrect. I thought he was a wise-cracking, fat old bollox and apart from referring to my brother Tom and myself as the 'Diddy men' when we played for Ireland together in 1968, I didn't know what else he thought of me. At any rate in 1978 fate threw us together and we developed an instant trust and liking for each other which has endured a lot of hassle and trauma over the years.

His concern for the players' well-being was the first characteristic I noted. He would literally do anything for them to make them settle down or prepare better for a game, and it was totally genuine and not feigned as is often the case. Players are good judges and they can spot a fake a long way off. Charades are not easily camouflaged.

When I suggested to Cud that the players should have top quality training and playing gear, stay and eat in the best hotels and have the best travel arrangements, he agreed readily and straightaway organised the Berkeley Court and the Royal Marine in Dun Laoghaire as our bases in Dublin for home games.

The players responded magnificently and their pride, self-worth and morale were launched into another dimension. Their response put Leinster rugby back where it belonged.

Cud also took great pride in organising the training venues and arrangements, refreshments and afterwards. I have fond memories of training evenings at Anglesea Road. He had a great sense of style and professionalism which his demeanour often belied but which rubbed off on everybody. He is most courteous, particularly towards women, and he made the players' girlfriends and wives enormously welcome into our rugby 'circus'.

He worked hard for Leinster and tried to get us as many quality games as he could. Cud was chairman of selectors for four of my five years with Leinster, and we built up an excellent working and social relationship in that time. We trusted each other's instincts implicitly and got on with what we had to do. While our exact duties were different, as we defined them, our responsibility for and involvement with the players overlapped and we did what we thought was either necessary or opportune at the time. The other selectors were a great bunch of guys who worked well together with all of us. We had no dissenters and had an awful lot of fun.

Some people might assume that The Cud and I were like the Mafia — hit men let loose on an unsuspecting rugby population of players and administrators: maybe we were. However, we were both very busy people in our everyday lives and we believed in getting things done without the prevarication and bullshit that often parades itself as in-depth thinking. We never colluded before a selection meeting — it would have been unfair and unproductive. We trusted the good sense and judgment of each selector and of each other. However, everyone knew what kind of player I wanted and the selection committee, nine times out of ten, would accede to my request.

Three relevant examples come easily to mind — the selection of George Wallace, Jim Glennon and Willie Duggan. None of them would be classified as lineout jumpers: in fact George and Jim could only jump from the shoulders up and Willie didn't get off the ground with the grace and athleticism of, say, a Michael Gibson. However, they were superb ball-winners and won as much possession as ever we wanted and made sure that it came back on our side to our advantage. That put them apart from the other contenders.

In 1983–4 in Thomond Park, George and Jim (Urbi et Orbi as we called them) totally eclipsed Mossy Keane and Donal Lenihan. Moss and Donal did the jumping but Urbi and Orbi did the business and won the ball. There is no player in his position that Willie Duggan couldn't take the ball from.

We used to practise positional play in lineouts and tactics to handle opposing lineout jumpers and we developed the call 'come dancing', at which signal our lineout men forcibly 'invited' their opposite number out to dance! It always worked. But these three guys were immensely strong and their ability in rucks, mauls and scrums was second to none. The Leinster selectors facilitated me with this intrepid trio from the outset and we were all rewarded.

Cud could become very emotional before games and as is his wont whenever he becomes excited, his mind runs slightly ahead of his speech. This of course led to many hilarious speeches and exhortations which the lads accepted in the spirit in which they were intended but would certainly have not tolerated from anyone else. Nobody else would have made them either.

I was on a farm call in Clonakility, Co. Cork when Lynne phoned me with the news of the awful accidental death of Meda Cuddy and the two darling girls. I got hold of Paddy Madigan later that evening who told me where to find Cud and made me promise that I would spend as much time as I could with Michael from now on especially during the early months of his bereavement. I tried to talk to him on the phone but couldn't — no words would come out. Solicitously he advised me to watch the treacherous roads and to mind myself on the way home — this at the height of his grief.

The funeral to Howth Cemetery was tragic, noble and heart-wrenching. The route from the church was lined with schoolfriends of the two girls.

In the months that followed we spent many an evening together. His capacity for self-control, even allowing for a measure of escapism, was inspiring, frightening and worrying. I kept in touch with Paddy Madigan and we discussed him a lot. Finally, one night as we were saying goodnight in the porch of the Old Wicklow Hotel, he broke down in my arms and all the pent-up grief, loneliness and awful sense of his enormous loss was able to drain out of him and I was happy for him that he didn't have to bottle it up anymore.

His immediate family were naturally supportive as were his mates and his sister-in-law, Ollie. His many close rugby and racing friends also lent their support. Most of all he developed a deep rapport with his son John and they became great friends. It was great to see.

After a while he met our friend Ms Helen Buckley B. Eng. — a young, vivacious, charming spinster whom he wooed with abandon and a few other things as well. Ms Buckley of Cloghan stole his heart away and they were married in Booterstown Avenue, in the church of course, in 1983. John gave his father away and made an incredibly witty speech afterwards. It was a beautiful day.

Unfortunately I had to curtail my festivities and drive to Donnybrook, late naturally, to supervise a Leinster squad session. At the previous session the lads had presented The Cud with a giant condom, a set of jump leads and an instruction manual. On this occasion I changed hastily behind a car and joined the squad session. One look at me and the lads knew I was in Disneyland. Every time I tried to stop them to address them they ran off to the far end of the pitch. After ten minutes of running around like this, the alcohol was coursing through every vein, artery and capillary so that I was truly knackered and I left them to their own devices.

I watched them from the Old Wesley bar with Thornton, Ging and Eric Campbell. It was observed of course that they seemed to be training better without me, the little buggers.

Cud and Helen have made a great couple and are truly well-matched. They now have a boy and a girl, Michael and Sarah and of course John Cuddy. Helen is a great girl and Mick is a lucky man. He keeps reminding me that if anything goes wrong it will have been my fault for introducing them. I know they'll always be happy together.

Early on, Helen knew that the memory of Meda and the girls was important to Cud and John. So she had all the photographs of the first family framed and given pride of place in their home. She knew that she didn't have to compete or obstruct The Cud's right to his wonderful, indelible memories. A truly superb woman who was lucky enough too, to meet her equal in a good man. Everyone who knows them loves being in their company.

The Cud earned the respect of the Leinster players, selectors and administrators who basked and revelled in his humour and all-embracing style. Not to mention the stream of malapropisms that stray from his lips from time to time. I think he invents them to confuse people.

I had hoped for the day when we might look after Ireland together because I knew we had the track record, self-assurance, reliance on each other and know-how to handle Irish players as we had done with Leinster. We had a brief spell of just one year at it together with Ireland and we made it count — boy, did we make it count. Many a man goes through life without a true guide, mentor and friend. I was lucky to meet Cud when I did. I suppose he was lucky also. OK, so we were both lucky!

Remembering it now, I am filled with nostalgia. I knew we both loved the players and looked after them as best we could. Part of their reaction is in the record books but the greater part of their response to us is in their eyes, their voices and salutations whenever we meet. In the end we were all helping each other and all of us created something special that we can be proud of — and we are. And to his credit, Michael Cuddy is responsible in large part for it.

After all, it was The Cud one night in July 1978 who took over an hour on the phone to persuade me to allow my name to go forward as Leinster coach. And that, as they say, was that.

10
Mandy — My Life Changes

'The story of my life is very clear to read,
It starts when you came in,
It ends whenever you leave'
(NEIL DIAMOND)

HER mother Sonia, once in 1978, threatened to have me and Toby, my black labrador, shot at dawn. Toby, because his nocturnal breaking and entering of Sonia's breeding kennels more often than not resulted in various new breeds of dogs like Lab-Shih-Tzu, Shiht-Labrador, Cocker-Labrador and Shihtador-Bichon. I was to be shot because I was his owner and couldn't control him. I agreed with Sonia to have Toby neutered but declined the operation myself. It was just as well — I married her daughter eleven years later!

It was on a blistering hot 58°F Irish summer's day with a force six gale whipping up a sandstorm at Brittas Bay, defying the application of my Factor 52, oil and water-proof, sun-proof, sand-proof and insect repellent cream, when I first clapped eyes on the ravishingly comely Amanda Power-Smith, a 26-year-old spinster and a pleasing wench forsooth.

I had returned the previous day from the Costa del Pubics in Tenerife after a languid, laid-back, hilarious piss-up of a holiday with my 'odd couple' partner, the one and only (and thank God there's only one) Thomas Mary Cleary. Lynne had gone off on her holidays, Andrew was with his grandparents the Thompsons in Somerset and so my two precious little ladies, Sharon and Amanda, prevailed on me

107

to drive them to stay with their pal, Emily Power-Smith at their summer retreat in Brittas Bay.

On my arrival at Costa del Bluetit I threaded my pristine black Saab, which Bobby Barden had persuaded me I urgently needed, through about 86 dogs of every shape, hue and cry; the whole of Westown Breeding Kennels were summering by the sea — a canine Cannes.

I found myself being introduced to the most serenely beautiful girl I had ever met — Mandy. I felt like an instant teenager meeting for the first time the girl of his dreams. To say that butterflies began to flutter in my stomach would be gross understatement: they began a reverse metamorphosis and turned back into caterpillars in the face of such loveliness.

Apart from that, she made me feel as randy as hell — her innocent bewitching eyes in conflict with the bolero top, bare midriff and the tightest pair of shorts ever sprouted by woman.

To confound my confusion, rising manhood and pulsating heart and wondering whether I should look or chastely avert my gaze, her two bolloxes of brothers Niall and Christopher were watching me, watching her, watching them.

Having established the fact that I liked dogs, I was offered a mug of tea and the freedom of Brittas Bay. I made a hit also with Granny — Mrs Molly Blanche Ellis — when she discovered that I like Jameson whiskey and donkeys (but not in the same glass). She was a true champion of helpless animals but sadly passed away in 1988. That was an enchanting week-end, a far, far cry from Playa de las Americas, Cleary's suntan and fear of tall women.

We all went for walks with the dogs along the beach — Sonia, Mandy, the three girls and myself — a forty-four-year-old teenager. I was completely smitten. We talked over a few drinks in the evening in McDaniel's Pub and despite the giggling and sniggering of the three pubescent young ladies, we gradually relaxed in each other's company. Her mother told me that she had a 'kind of' a boyfriend but that she didn't love him.

My daughters had an incredible rapport with Mandy — she had come home a lot at weekends over the years and they got to know her well — and she them. Her sister Emily was in school in Alexandra College with them and they had been playmates for years. We had lived about 400 yards apart all these years and I had never met Mandy until 1984 even though there was quite a lot of contact between the two families.

As a consequence of all that I felt both nervous and shy about asking Mandy out; also I was afraid, I suppose, of our age difference — eighteen years— and of being rebuffed. I had come through a traumatic and painful few years since my separation from Lynne and the confidence department was very suspect. I had to await the exact, correctly-timed opportunity to achieve my desired aim — a date with Mandy.

I had gone out with a nice girl called Helen a few times during the early summer and had asked her to go to the Neil Diamond concert in Croke Park with me in July. This was now a problem. The inventive part of me decided that I should ask Mandy to come to see Neil Diamond with me and call it off with Helen. I asked young Emily if she thought Mandy would go if I asked her and Emily said she'd be delighted to'. I cautioned her not to mention it to Mandy knowing full well and hoping she would, of course. And she did, bless her. Emily, I owe you!

Anyway she accepted, to my natural delight. But now I had to tell Helen. I admit I behaved like a louse albeit for the first and only time in my life. I waited until the afternoon of the concert and phoned her to say that I was stranded in Clonakilty and couldn't get back in time. The concert was fabulous — all the nostalgia was tear-provoking and the songs — *Cracklin' Rosie, Travelling Salvation Show, Holly Holy* and all those wonderful lyrics. After an hour I ventured to hold Mandy's hand and gave her a peck on the cheek after two hours.

On the way home I met Johnny and Deirdre Cantrell and joined them at their Lansdowne Road pad for drinks and a take-away.

We danced to some Santana music at John and Deirdre'
until sex, love, lust, passion, tenderness and exquisite pair
overcame us and we repaired to Mandy's house in Baggo
Lane. It was the most completely happy night of my life and
all the sensual, physical, psychological wonderful rivers o
emotions and feelings that can flow between a man and a
woman, drive them to ride the rapids of love and bathe ir
the mental moonlight of calming waters — all these feeling
and thoughts and sensations fused into absolute harmony
and I for one was at peace for the first time in my life. I had
found MY woman and nothing on this earth was going to
take her away from me.

I had found the previous three years of living on my own
awfully lonely and had broached with Maria, by letter, the
idea of getting back together in some way. However the
arrival of Mandy cancelled everything and Maria and mysel
had a very friendly, enjoyable dinner in the Lord Edward
(one of my all-time favourites) and an amicable parting. I'n
glad that she is now happily remarried and has found her
own peace.

My children were delighted, and my son Andrew though
Mandy was a grand bird. My great friend Olivia Keaveney
approved wholeheartedly. Olivia has helped me to keep life
in true perspective ever since I've known her from 1971. She
is a true blue. Lynne was very happy for me if a little surprised
and bemused. The last of the big swingers had succumbed.

The 'baby snatcher' accusation even got an airing. As we
gradually began to go out together and meet our friends, both
our lives began to take shape and thankfully all our inner
most secret feelings, the ones we all have but are mostly afraid
to reveal in order to avoid serious hurt, began to take root
emerge, and flourish.

I was enthralled to discover that our hidden private selve
mirrored each other, having no need or room for pretence
or concealment. Of course this rapidly dispelled the hurt and

pain we had both felt from previous experiences and the healing hands of time massaged us until the mutual confidence
in a close relationship kindled and took fire.

Indeed the lines of a favourite Willie Nelson song, courtesy
of Hugh Gibson of Omagh, often came to mind:

> 'They're working, while I'm missing you
> Those healing hands of time,
> Soon, they'll be dismissing you,
> Those healing hands of time.
> Already I've reached mountain peaks
> and I've just begun to climb.
> I know I'll get over you, by clinging to
> Those healing hands of time.'

I came to realise that time is the master healer and what-
ever He, Whose gift time is, allows to befall us in our lives,
He and only He can send us the healing hand that saves us.
Somebody sent Mandy to me — of that I have no doubt.
Something omniscient propelled me towards her and my
children provided the time and the meeting place.

Rugby and my close friends ensured my survival, mental
stability and physical health during the lonely years after
Lynne and Maria. I had taken up jogging fairly seriously
around 1980 and without a doubt it was instrumental in
saving my life. I had, as mentioned earlier, begun to drink
heavily and more consistently around the time of my marriage break-up. I had been teetotal until I was twenty-eight
years of age but I made up for it subsequently. I have always
enjoyed a good jar and I like social drinking. But when it
gets to the stage where you have to drink to get a good buzz
going quickly then drink is taking over and becoming a
serious mental and physical health hazard.

Suffice to say that when the good ship Mandy landed on
my lonely island I was good and ready for her. I really felt
like a nineteen-year-old on his first date. I almost expected

to have to ask somebody's permission to go out with her
Can you imagine that?

Your first sweetheart has a special place in your life and is
a bench mark by which you make comparisons in subsequent
relationships. The awakening feelings of being a grown man,
the expectations, the innocence, the planning and dreaming
and the developing of self-belief are the hallmarks of a first
love affair. Added to this is the trust, the caring, and the
putting oneself second in the hierarchy of importance in a
close relationship.

All that had been lost for me until I met Mandy in July
1984 and immediately I was transported back to 1959 —
twenty-five years earlier and my first love. I was free and not
afraid anymore. With Mandy I was back spiritually to my teenage years but with a big, big difference — experience and
the wisdom of age. I had learned a lot in the intervening
twenty five years — especially from my relationship and
marriage with Lynne and my expedition with Maria.

I had been hurt more deeply than I realised. I had been
lonely and almost desperate but luckily I had not become
embittered, or blamed anyone but myself for what befell me.
My friend, Dave Geaney, veterinary surgeon, from Castleisland, Co. Kerry once gave me very good advice when he
gave me my first job as a vet in 1964. 'Mike', said Dave, 'Use
your eyes and ears. A wise man learns by observation, a
fucking eejit learns by experience.'

I hope observation has prevailed over experience. It was
only when I was alone, and I mean totally, unequivocally alone
that I began to understand women fully and the simple but
complex nature of our relationships with them — role-playing
being the major deterrent to a good relationship, and the cause
of more misunderstanding and pain than any other factor.

By the time I met Mandy I had identified and rationalised
all the areas in which I had either fallen down or otherwise
not lived up to my own or others' expectations of me. I had re-

solved not to repeat those mistakes if I was ever lucky enough to meet a good woman again. I had explored the minefield of role-playing and I had learned to keep the argumentative side of me and my explosive short-fused temper in some control.

I have a quick temper — I am easily wound up over specific things. However my temper is of the verbally expressive kind and lasts about 15–30 seconds during which time I try to get as many fucks, bolloxes, and bejaysuses as possible into my apoplectic, imaginative, incoherent ramblings. Thankfully I never struck a girl or a woman in my life (I've been sorely tempted mind you) nor have I ever beaten my children. On the football pitch I will gladly, for the right reason, knock some fucker's head off if I have to but that's fair game — fit sportsmen are an equal match for each other. I think it is indefensible, cowardly and lacking in all sense of fair play, humanity and manly behaviour for any man to beat up, batter or ever strike women and children. Real men don't do it. There is no excuse — absolutely no excuse for such pathological behaviour.

There is no point in arguing that the social climate, the jobless mess, the recession, the housing shortage or any other reason is the cause of violent male behaviour towards women and children. The cause is basic, bloody ignorance whose roots lie in an education system and a religious system that singularly fail to teach children respect for the other sex. Nor does it prepare boys and girls, before they develop unhealthy attitudes towards each other, for the serious but enjoyable business of living together as life partners, lovers, husbands and wives and bringing up their own families and contributing something positive to the world.

A man's obligation is to love, cherish and look after his wife and children to the best of his ability, not to abuse them or make them his servants or to dominate or bully them. A lot of men need to do a lot of growing up — fast. It is an insult to human intelligence, and a wrong that screams out to be righted, to see and hear of the unspeakable sufferings of countless women and children in modern society.

Here the Catholic Church, which claims 96% of the Republic's citizens as followers, has a job to do. It should rid itself of its self-induced guilt complexes about human sexuality and stop passing on its negative ideas about the psychological and biological facts of life — ideas as relevant as a fart in a wet suit — and concentrate on positives like inculcating children with proper respect for and understanding of love between the sexes. If it did, we would be well on the way to the starting blocks, and in a fit state to *begin* to learn and understand our differing natures and how they can complement each other.

Anyway, by the time I met Mandy I had washed myself clear of my immature assumptions about my role as a male partner. When we saw our relationship ripening and developing into something wonderful we sort of gravitated to living together. We made a fairly simple but important decision. We resolved *never* to become angry with one another, or to fight or raise our voices in anger.

It has worked wonderfully well for us but requires self-discipline, good will and commitment. We have been together now since 1984 in a very close one-to-one relationship and we are very happy, thank God.

This does not mean of course that we don't get on each others' wick from time to time or feel like neutering one another. Of course we do. We are both short-tempered but we keep our mouths shut. It you don't say it you won't regret it. If you do say it you can't take it back.

Mandy was, and is, a revelation. In the early months of our relationship we went to the movies, rock concerts, swimming, jogging, drinking and everything else in life that is enjoyable and ends in -ing!

She is the sweetest, gentlest, most serene, unhurried person I have ever met and she brings calm, order and meaning to my life. She was, in 1984, a new lease of new life to me, and having only met her briefly I wanted to commit my whole life to her — body and soul. My children, particularly Sharon and Amanda, were the first to realise how compatible and 'simpatico' Mandy and I were. They were quite intrigued that their Dad, their old man, was going out with a friend of theirs. What was most important was that they approved and spent a lot of time in our company. I was transported with happiness, naturally — I had met the woman I had always sought and discovered that my feelings and dreams were reciprocated.

Around the middle of July 1984 I won the selectors' vote for the job of Irish rugby coach and so began together the two love affairs of my life — Mandy and Irish international rugby. The interviews began the day after the vote — Karl Johnston and Sean Diffley had heard the rumours and had deduced quite a few facts for themselves. Two cute hoors, the pair of them!

My relationship with Mandy had an enormous bearing on my tenure as Irish coach. She gave me the love and affection and the quality of life and support that I needed to allow me to give myself completely to the players in my charge and to the other people who put their trust in me, not to mention the Irish public who supported us.

It is patently obvious that a sound, loving relationship is a pre-requisite to success in other fields. With the Irish rugby scene Mandy fitted in well with the players' girlfriends and wives. She was, after all, the same age as most of them, and she was mature enough to synchronise with the senior wives of the IRFU entourage, some of whom like Helen Cuddy and Joan Boyle were also quite young and beautiful.

It was heartwarming to experience the genuine affection rugby people had for me and the lengths to which they went to make Mandy feel at home and relaxed in their company. In short, we were accepted as a couple and this made everything to do with the next three incident-filled years more enjoyable and worthwhile.

We moved house in August from Pinewood Lodge at Poulaphouca in Wicklow to Sherlockstown Lodge in Sallins, Co. Kildare where we began to collect our menagerie of dogs and make plans.

Pinewood Lodge was a lovely house overlooking the lakes in a beautiful wooded setting — 'sylvan' as the estate agents would call it. I had lived there on my own for a year before I met Mandy and all the neighbours who had grown accustomed to seeing me beating a lone track around the roads on my early morning jogs were quite impressed with my new vertical jogging companion and the 'get ups' she had wormed herself into. The hand waves and the tooting of horns wasn't for me obviously — the people of the lakes were blaring and trumpeting their approval of my choice of pacemaker and envied me the view of the lovely nubile bottom in front of me framed by the lakes and trees.

I honestly think I was the first person to pole vault around the lakes on all fives.

We moved our jogging routine to Sherlockstown with much the same effect on passing motorists. One could almost hear through partly open car windows cries of 'baby snatcher', 'sex maniac' and other such complimentary remarks.

Anyway we settled here in Sherlockstown in a lovely, peaceful area with a superb view of the Wicklow hills and mountains. And we settled into a regular pattern. I dropped Mandy off at her father, Niall's house at Johnstown and they travelled to Dublin together every morning. She worked as his secretary in his Chartered Quantity Surveyor's business — A. Edward Smith & Co. — and she came home with him in the evenings. It was a lovely, regular routine from the start and it lent a feeling of permanence to our life together.

It provided a safe haven from the rugby madness that was to take over our lives for the next three years. I had found my own oasis in Mandy. I was the luckiest man I knew.

11
Ireland 1984–5 — Giving
It A Lash

'A long, long time ago, I can still remember
How the music used to make me smile,
And I knew if I had my chance,
that I could make those people dance,
And maybe they'd be happy for a while . . .'
(DON McLEAN — AMERICAN PIE)

AS the advertising hoarding proclaims of the latest GTXI: Twin Cam Boxer engined four-wheel drive steed — 'If you have it, flaunt it.'

I knew we had 'it' and I also knew that we would flaunt it whenever we could. The 'it' was the individual and collective talent that was available in Irish rugby in the autumn of 1984. Five years of deep interprovincial involvement had given me a fairly thorough insight into the real talent available. Of course there were problems: Ollie Campbell, Fergus Slattery, Willie Duggan, Colm Tucker, Robbie McGrath, John O'Driscoll, Moss Keane were either retired or not available, and this was a fair chunk of players to remove almost at one stroke from any national team. But there were also opportunities. We had some good old hands still remaining: Philip Orr, Ciaran Fitzgerald, Mick Fitzpatrick, Donal Lenihan, Moss Finn, Trevor Ringland, Hugo MacNeill and Michael Kiernan. There was also a new crop of young, fit, talented players waiting in the wings dying to be asked to join the action.

The previous year Ireland had lost all its matches ignominiously and none as badly as the last game against Scotland.

The team was dispirited throughout the campaign and was without direction or motivation.

Ciaran Fitzgerald had been dropped after the Welsh game and Willie Duggan was elected captain — a role he didn't want and for which he had no experience. Willie could have been a good captain on the field, but the after-dinner speaker bit didn't excite him much. He and I worked on his speech before the England-Ireland dinner in London 1984. Reckoning that the main body of people at this stag dinner would be well-oiled and very amenable to rapid self-effacing humour we decided that Willie should begin his speech thus: 'Gentlemen of England and Ireland, standing before you makes one feel as the cock-pheasant must have done when asked to present the prize to the best shot at the start of the shooting season!' We felt that this would hit the right note. The idea then was that Willie would say his next few words quickly and be seated before the rabble knew that he had even stood up to speak.

To say that Willie fluffed his lines would be misleading. He cocked them up completely. He stood up and mumbled to his neighbour, 'Is this mike live?' and began: 'Ladies and Gentlemen', (pause) 'Oh fuck it, I've made a bollox of it already!' With Mossy Keane's noisy encouragement, Willie continued sportingly to the end and received a standing boo.

Willie manfully agreed to become in effect the fall guy: incredibly in some circles he is regarded as the cause of the failure of that year's team. Far from it! I was a sub-selector that year. Roly Meates was chairman of selectors, Willie John McBride was coach and a selector, as were Jim Donaldson, Brian O'Brien and Mick Cuddy. The team was poorly prepared for its games and the loss of Fitzie was a huge demoralising blow. The departure of Ollie Campbell and Fergus Slattery was also incalculable. I spent quite a while with Willie Duggan, at his request, privately working out lineout and other strategies.

The evening after the Scottish game in Dublin was sad. The team had played poor pointless rugby all season and were in abject misery. The following morning I met Willie Duggan and Moss Keane. They confided that they were both retiring from representative rugby and I was sad for them — they deserved a better, more fitting stage from which to make their exit into rugby history. They urged me to take over the Irish team management and to give it back its pride, advice which fell on willing ears. I had listened to the other players that sad morning in Foley's pub and it had fired me with a burning determination to take over, despite the predictable odium and criticism which would come my way.

I decided over that weekend that I would not wait another three years for my chance to look after these players. I resolved to handle whatever flak I would surely receive from predictable sources and use the IRFU's own preferred system of democratic selection that I have already described. I am glad that I did, and so are a lot of other people — especially players. I sought the advice of serious rugby people all over Ireland and was heartened by the overwhelmingly positive response to the unprecedented action I had prepared myself to take. Two friends suggested in good faith that I should let Willie John have another year.

Let me depict the scenario. Willie John McBride, the legendary Irish and Lions player and captain, had been elected Irish coach for the 1983–4 season. He was one of five selectors who at that time chose the coach from a list of names submitted by the coaching subcommittee of the IRFU. Willie John's name and mine went before that selection committee in July 1983. Willie had coached Ulster for one season a year previously and had just returned as a chastened manager from an underwhelming Lions Tour to New Zealand. By July 1983, I had coached Leinster for four successful seasons and felt that I had earned my coaching stripes for the Irish team job.

However Willie John, being a selector, had a vote and I didn't. Willie, Jim Donaldson (Ulster) and Roly Meates (Leinster) voted for Willie John with Brian O'Brien (Munster) and Michael Cuddy (Leinster) voting for me. I was naturally disappointed but we had reckoned in advance that Meates would not vote for me. McBride, Donaldson and Meates had also voted Meates in as chairman. Ireland went on to have an awful 1983–4 season, without the saving grace of even one decent performance. In July 1984 Jim Kiernan (Munster) replaced Brian O'Brien and I replaced Roly Meates as full selectors. Johnny Moroney (Munster) and Eddie Coleman (Leinster) were the sub-selectors. Benny O'Dowd (Bohemians) was unceremoniously axed in the process but Cuddy and myself couldn't be blamed for that.

During the early summer of 1984 I discussed the consequences of my proposed action with Brian, Michael Cuddy and Jim Kiernan. The Cud, true to form, saw the logic of what could happen but said to me 'Doyler, you and I have been mates for a long time now and you know that this is my last chance to be chairman.' He made it crystal clear to me that if his support for me as coach was likely to screw up his chances of being chairman, I could forget about it!

Jim Kiernan was the key and I put the proposition fairly and squarely to him. 'Jim, if you think I would be Irish coach and will support me with your vote I will run. If not, I will not allow my name to go forward to a vote so as to make Willie John the uncontested unanimous choice.' Jim replied, 'Mick, I want you to be the Irish coach but with Cuddy and yourself, two Leinstermen, in charge it could be a recipe for disaster.'

'But Jim' I said, 'I'm a Kerryman!' 'Yeah', says Jim, 'but you're not a Munster man!' Rugby-wise he was correct. He enquired if I could work with Willie John should he be elected chairman of selectors. I replied, 'No problem'. (Brian Lenihan would have approved.)

And so the die was cast and the stage was set for an eventful meeting in July 1984 to elect a chairman of selectors and a coach. Ronnie Dawson, representing the Union committee, supervised the selection of chairman. Jim Kiernan proposed Willie John for chairman and said, 'I want Mick Doyle to be Irish coach.'

I proposed Michael Cuddy for chairman and Ronnie visibly blanched at what was unfolding. Willie John said that he wasn't interested in being chairman so Jim Kiernan then seconded Michael Cuddy's nomination. Unbelievably it still went to a vote; we had a secret ballot to select a chairman from two nominees, one of whom didn't want to run. Cuddy won the vote 3–2. Ronnie Dawson then withdrew. Cud took the chair and welcomed Roly Meates as the representative of the IRFU coaching sub-committee. Meates proposed two names for consideration as Irish coach — Willie John McBride and Michael Doyle, 'in no particular order' as he told Jim Kiernan, but added that the committee had recommended 'no change'.

Chairman Cuddy thanked him for the two names but pointed out that the committee didn't have a brief to make a recommendation supporting either man.

Meates withdrew and Michael Cuddy fairly and meticulously proceeded with the serious business of electing a coach. He gave Willie John and myself adequate time to 'state our cases' and fully develop our themes. Cud, unlike the rest of us then, was, and is still a respected member of the IRFU committee and will be president, please God, in the 1992–3 season. He was obliged, of course, to ensure a fair selection under the terms of the IRFU's own selection procedures and he behaved impeccably.

I won't dwell on Willie John's and my own points of view as expressed to the other selectors except to emphasise that our views on coaching Ireland were diametrically opposed. Jim Donaldson and Jim Kiernan spoke on the merits of Willie and myself respectively.

I was elected by 3 votes to 2. I was elated but touched by sadness for Willie John's hurt and my own anger at the system that created all that humiliating hassle. There was no way that this rugby 'gunfight at the OK Corral' should ever have taken place; it was an insult to all five people concerned. In effect, the system had failed in the summer of 1983. By July 1983 I had concluded the four most successful seasons in Leinster's 100-year history including the then unprecedented three interprovincial titles in a row. In the process I learned the art and craft of managing players and developing an exciting game with them; if that is coaching, then I would be deemed to have been a success. I had served my time.

By July 1983 Willie John had spent just one year learning to coach Ulster. He had a superb track record as a player and captain; he was a grand man, likeable, funny, an excellent team mate and companion. I had played twenty consecutive games for Ireland with him from 1964 to 1969, had toured Australia with him in 1967 and South Africa in 1968. I knew an awful lot about Willie John McBride. I liked him immensely, I admired him greatly and I respected him completely. But in 1983 he was in no way ready to coach Ireland. He had very little real close team and man management experience at representative level with Ulster and had just returned from a traumatic tour of New Zealand as Lions manager. He had been making progress with a young Ulster team who were responding to him but this was disrupted when he accepted management of the Lions.

The transition from team captain to coach had been as difficult for him as it would have been for me or for anyone else in similar circumstances. Logic and planning would have suggested that Willie would have profited from two or three years breathing space with Ulster and then been able to handle Ireland quite readily.

Coaching Ireland should not be a reward for past services rendered, nor a recognition for one's contribution as a player. A proven track record as a coach is a prime essential, allied to the ability to man-manage, motivate and develop a team. Willie John was catapulted into the coaching job far too soon. In 1983 I certainly felt let down and aggrieved. I lost that year because I couldn't vote. I won in 1984, not just because I had a vote, but because Jim Kiernan had the courage and foresight to do the right thing.

That is the true, factual account of how I eventually became Irish coach.

I am proud of what I did and glad I did it. I would do exactly the same again under similar circumstances if I had to. It was never anything personal between me and Willie John. Anything suspected to the contrary is dishonest and false and an insult to both of us. So now you know!

Understandably the flak arrived but I had The Cud beside me and I had always preserved a good set of neck muscles — and I needed them a lot over the next three years. It was an exciting time. I'd just become Irish coach, the position I respect most in Irish rugby apart from the team captain, and I had met the girl that Santa Claus had always told me he would bring me when I was good and ready. I was ready and I was good too.

We had developed an open democratic society in Leinster rugby and had evolved our own formula of consultation, commitment, decision and action. So Cud and I travelled around the provinces' early season games and training sessions and put it into practice on a wider front. We spoke directly to the players. We told them that there were many places available on the Irish team, that selection would be on merit, that we needed dedication and commitment. Players were made aware that if they turned up at our training sessions unfit they would be sent home. Personal fitness was their problem. My concern was how to utilise all the skills available and build the best team we could. I decided to develop a game style that the players were most happy with and to which they would give 100% commitment.

The Connacht squad was our first stop on a windswept Sunday in September in Castlebar. Cud said to me before we went in, 'Doyler, what do you want me to say?' I replied that he should explain that our methods were well-known and fair and that we would guarantee equality to every player. He did very well and got his message across — in his anxiety he nearly choked himself by twisting his tie around his neck nervously, an endearing little idiosyncrasy.

I dwelt upon aspirations of rugby players, the example that Ciaran Fitz had been to all players and the need for players to make the extra effort this year for a new Irish team. The lads' response was good and Connacht played its part, as always, in getting the best Irish team out to play.

We went to Ravenhill the next night and spoke to the Ulster players after their training session with Jimmy Davidson. Cud, speaking first, upstaged me and delivered the homily that I had given the day before, the bollox. I had to change my emphasis and concentrate on specifics. I zeroed in on Willie Anderson, a player and a bloke for whom I had and have the utmost regard, and pointed out that he should have had about ten or so caps by 1984. The Ulster players agreed with me and even though I had replaced their own Willie John as Irish coach they, to a man, gave me their full support, trust and loyalty over the three years that I was involved with them.

They also supplied a large number of good players and some great players to our team in this period. On the way back, we stopped at Bill Mulligan's Half Way House near Banbridge to have a meal and a few jars. We became entangled, gladly I might add, in the tail-end of a funeral; there was so much crack and jollity you'd have thought it was a wedding reception. I told a few yarns and Cud brought the house and the table down with his inimitable rendition of *McNamara's Band* in Braille and Swahili as well.

In typically Irish fashion we travelled to London to talk to Munster players! They were playing Surrey at the London-

Irish grounds and we had a word with them — and Jim Kiernan had a word or two with us over a few pints.

We spoke to the Leinster players during a squad session with Ned Thornton in Belfield. The lads were impressed by The Cud's new air of seriousness and took the piss out of both of us. Cud upstaged me again in London and Dublin delivering my previous day's script verbatim (and word for word too). I resolved never to allow him to speak before me again or else to demand to see his prepared script in advance.

However we knew what we meant and I think the players knew it also; they believed and trusted us. They knew from our track record with Leinster that we said what we meant and meant what we said. Truth and honesty are the first and last principles of trust — at times it may not suit but nevertheless the requirement is always there. I detest prevarication and waffle.

Whether people liked Cuddy or myself was immaterial really. While we all want to be liked, we were happy that no-one was under any illusion about what we were up to and all players knew exactly where they stood with us. We gave them our best and if it wasn't good enough — so be it.

Our selection committee of Willie John, Jim Donaldson, Jim Kiernan and myself with chairman Cud included Eddie Coleman and Johnny Moroney as sub-selectors. They had an equal voice to full selectors but only the five voted. In this way the sub-selectors had a quite important role in that they could be much more expansive and adventurous in their opinions. This was often needed to silence the scourge of conservatism or, translated into plain English, the fear of being wrong, of making the wrong decision, or not making any bloody decision. Why are conservatives more concerned with being right? It baffles me. Why do they waffle on and on without getting to the real point?

Our committee met regularly in the early 1984–5 season and picked a very big squad of about 48 players based really on past experience. We had our first baptism as an Irish team against Australia in October and we hadn't much time to prepare. In some of the early season's games we had noted Mick Kiernan's ability to kick goals from anywhere and we had arranged with some understanding friends in Connacht, notably P.J. Dwyer and Ollie Burke, to have Paul Dean selected at outhalf for a few games.

P.J. Dwyer asked me down to Athlone to 'coach' the 'rest' team against Connacht. Deano was at outhalf and was great. That was the first time that I had seen Noel Mannion: Owen Hosty introduced us afterwards. I'm glad he has made it — he still has a good future in rugby ahead of him if he concentrates on more specific aspects of his game.

Cud and I were adamant that Fitzie would be our captain and that Paul Dean would be our outhalf. The other selectors agreed totally and we picked what we felt was the best team available to play Australia. After the team was selected of course, the real talking point was not so much the selection of Paul Dean but the omission of Tony Ward. Mick Bradley's selection was questioned from the same quarters. I phoned Brad and told him that we were proud to have him on our team. All the usual plethora of fatigued expressions were offered but we had decided that we had had enough of the one man band syndrome and selected Paul Dean because of what he could offer the players in front of and outside him and we didn't give a tuppeny curse whether he could drop goals, kick converts or not. We knew we had Michael Kiernan, Moss Finn, Hugo MacNeill and Mick Bradley if we needed them. After all Tom Kiernan had a most incredible run at full back for Ireland and he rarely kicked a goal that mattered; or he couldn't be depended on to do so. His unrivalled occupancy of the full back position on the Irish team for so long was because he was the best full back available as well as being an excellent captain.

Deano was my choice for outhalf — he was not an established outhalf or even a notable kicker. Tony Ward and Ollie Campbell had been vying for the No. 10 place for years and various experimental combinations had been tried, albeit half-heartedly, to accommodate both these great players together on the Irish team. Had I been in charge, and with The Cud and an enlightened team of selectors, I certainly would have pursued the 5/8 option often used by New Zealand to great effect. The problem of course, was that there were centres in Ireland at the time who were far better than either Ollie or Tony in this position — like Ian Burns! With Ollie's premature retirement our choices were between Tony and Paul Dean.

I would dearly love to have been involved with Tony Ward at the start of his representative career, both inter-provincial and international. A player of his gifted football talents needed serious, strong direction — especially in exploring and expanding the full scope of his repertoire. His talents were often under-utilised in the interests of expediency. He was mostly left isolated and made responsible for the direction of the game and the pattern of team play. Premature media adulation and unrealistic expectations of him created the one man band phenomenon which attracted enormous pressures which are difficult to rationalise. He was being expected to do everything and he responded body and soul to this role and lost himself. The mantle of real, charismatic superstardom landed easily and too early on his youthful shoulders.

All players need a mentor — one who is sympathetic, informed and unselfish. The superstars need even more such support, not less. I don't believe that Wardie had that solid back-up — he often appeared to me to be a lonely figure, operating very much on his own and being continually misunderstood. Obviously, his bombshell dropping in Australia without the benefit of wise counselling as it were, impacted deeply and negatively on him and his life, and his game went to pieces.

I went for Deano because of his incredible hands and his ability to get the best out of players outside him. I assessed that Tony Ward's pattern of play had become engrained and that I wouldn't be able to alter it in a short space of time. Tony was in our squad, naturally, but our first choice was Paul.

In 1986 against Scotland Wardie played one of the best games I had ever seen him play — he adapted to our type of play and had a most complete afternoon. It made me sad for what might have been. In latter years, his life, like mine, has taken on new meaning. He began to enjoy his work, his rugby and his journalism. He married his Louise and he now lives happily with her and their family. He is more and more a composed, total person, one whom it is a joy to meet. We are now journalistic mates and find that we have so many things in common and have been able to dispel many of the misconceptions we were supposed to hold about one another — shades of Cud and myself, revisited. However, I would still pick Deano if I was starting off again and for the same reasons, all things else being equal. What I would have done had all three — Ollie, Wardie and Deano — been available, I don't honestly know. Committed suicide, picked three outhalves, took up sevens, I haven't a clue. I won't be losing any sleep now anyway.

I was lucky to have been involved with three such enormous talents as well as three such fabulous human beings. Very few people are that privileged. I learned a lot from all three of them.

Cud and I invited Ciaran Fitzgerald to meet us one evening in the Berkeley Court Hotel — in the bar, naturally. Neither of us knew the man very well and he was wary of us. We wanted to put his mind at rest at once and give him the authority and visibly tangible backing that every captain needs to function properly.

We were cognisant of the fact that he had been badly let down in '84 by Ireland and that on the 1983 Lions tour in

New Zealand he had been vilified by the British rugby press (who else?). Obviously he was going to react cautiously to honeyed words from people he did not know well. However he trusted us and took us at our word. None of us regretted that, I am glad to say.

I asked Fitzie if he would like to go to see Australia play England. He thought I was mad. The Cud knew what I was at and off he went without a word to phone George Spottswood to arrange for Fitzie, Jim Kiernan and myself to travel to London the next week. Ciaran couldn't believe it. It was not pre-planned and had occurred to me as the first tangible thing that Cud and I could do to show Fitzie that he was part of our management team and every bit as important as any of us. That was the first time an Irish captain had ever been asked to go to watch the opposition. Of course it makes sense: it is vital that the captain and coach jointly assess their next opposition in the flesh. That set the benchmark for our relationship and the show was on the road.

The following year, The Cud had gone, and my request for Fitzie to travel to Scotland with me to watch Scotland v. France was refused. I refused to travel and threatened to make public my reasons if Ciaran was not with me. We did travel to Edinburgh together: the conservatives surrendered. It didn't do us much good, mind you. The French hockeyed us in Paris but that's another story.

We prepared well for Australia. We trained in Suttonians' ground in Sutton before the game and had our first meal together as a team the night before in the Marine Hotel. Charles J. Haughey phoned Fitzie and myself to wish us the best of luck. He was in opposition then.

The night before the game or at least about 4 a.m. on Saturday morning Ned Thornton's phone-call woke me up. 'Doyler', says Ned, 'Yer man Ella has only one foot!' He meant, of course, that he could kick only with his left foot. 'Tell me more', I said. I got a bottle of Bacardi and a six pack of Coke and a bucket of ice from the fridge, as well as pencil and paper and settled down to a two-hour unravelling of the Aussies' game. We changed our tactics to measure up to Thornton's hard information. He said I owed him for the bottles of brandy which had helped lubricate his Australian informant.

The other Ned in my life, Ned Van Esbeck, had spotted my Ned at the Australian training session and put two and two together.

As it turned out we nearly won. We could have won if we had had the experience of even one match together. It was a great game and a pointer to things to come. I was enormously proud of my players, even in defeat, and I knew our philosophy was right. We said to all and sundry that we would 'give it a lash' and we kept our word.

The Irish rugby aficionados and rugby public accepted our promise and responded superbly to what we tried to do. The press, sceptical at first, began to see that we meant business and that we were all committed to 15-man attacking rugby and nothing else.

I have always been up front about anything I think, do or say and I took a lot of time to explain to the rugby journalists what we were trying to achieve and how we would play. I emphasised that we should be judged on performance not on results: if our performance was right the results would look after themselves.

The rugby media had generally been reporting a game that the players were not playing; I decided to be as frank and as complete as I could with them without giving away our trade secrets. Cud, Fitzie and myself were available to answer any questions of relevance and sometimes of no relevance. The media are the people who carry the message to the paying public and have a very important position within the game.

The rugby-playing public are the people who pay for the game and who keep it going. Without their interest and support, the game is an irrelevance. Therefore, I believed then and I believe now that the public who support us, our team and our game deserve to get something to shout about — they are due their money's worth.

Any team which lines up in a green jersey will get the most committed, unselfish, least critical support of any nation on earth and all they ask in return is value for money. They want to be proud of Ireland and the Irish team — win, lose, or draw! The result is not the main consideration; neither is rugby theory or dogma of any relevance. We knew that with our players we could win half our matches but that even when we lost we would always give a good account of ourselves and keep our pride and that of our supporters and friends high.

In November 1984 we beat a strong Scottish B side in Galway. Our team was captained by Declan Fanning, the Leinster captain, who did a superb job of leadership on an awful day. Ralph Keyes gave a youthful, inexperienced Gavin Hastings a bellyful of Garryowens and Nigel Carr was waiting for them when they returned to earth. Brian McCall and Matt D'Arcy played proverbial blinders. The Irish team was delighted — most of them had been humiliated by almost the same Scottish XV in Scotland the previous year.

The Lady Mayor, Bridie O'Flaherty, held a reception for both teams on the Friday afternoon. When I had organised my warriors and chaired the final team talk with them I collected Derek Grant, the Scottish coach and an old adversary and friend from playing days and his assistant Doug Morgan. We went out to Moran's of the Weir and had a few pints of Chateau Saunders to wash down a few hundred oysters, crab claws and the like. We discussed everything but rugby — there was no point discussing the game because we were going to win anyway!

Cud's exhortations to the men in green before the game in the dressing room would have brought tears to the eyes of an undertaker — tears of laughter, that is. He was hilarious without even trying. By the time he was finished with whatever he wanted the lads to do to the Scots I wouldn't have been at all surprised had the Scots refused to play.

Two weeks later, minutes before the start of the Leinster v. Connacht interprovincial game, The Cud, with me in tow, again entered the green dressing room to exhort his men to deeds of valour and questionable ethics. Michael Tarpey, the Connacht second row, told Cud in the nicest possible way that he was in the wrong dressing room, that he should be talking to his own Leinster players and to stop making a nuisance of himself. Cud departed in his own time expressing the hope that Leinster would beat the shit out of them. I'll never forget the look of utter incredulity on the Connacht players' faces as The Cud began to address them.

The final trial in December produced Brian Spillane and confirmed Nigel Carr's pre-eminence among loose forwards. It also told us that we had an excellent squad of well-balanced players. Some connoisseurs pointed out that our scrums weren't great: they were right. To those people of open minds who are willing to listen I will reiterate — the scrums, like line outs, kick-offs and twenty-two drop outs are a method of restarting the game: they are not ends in themselves. They can become ends in themselves with certain types of very heavy packs.

Because the side putting in the ball has the loose or free head, their hooker is always nearer the ball than his rival and thus 99% of the time his side will win the ball. Timing the shove, position of feet, synchronisation of mind and body between eight forwards and the scrum half is of more importance than brute strength.

With the Leinster pack we knew we had a better pack than even most current national sides and we used our huge superiority in scrums properly with intelligent half backs calling the shots.

With the Ireland squad in 1984–5 we knew we did NOT have a strong scrummaging pack and any long concentrated scrummaging sessions would not provide a justifiable return — in other words we wouldn't have become much better and we would have over-emphasised the importance of the scrum. In twenty-odd games, only the French in Paris in 1986 and England in 1986 in Twickenham on the frozen pitch at both ends near our line had outscrummed us. In Paris the French destroyed us. For Twickenham, the selectors got it wrong and the balance of our front and second rows was destroyed; Paul Kennedy was selected at loose head on the team and England knew that he wasn't even a loose head!

My priority in 1984, from the outset, and the wish of the players, selectors and obviously, the public was to develop the most suitable game for our young, fit, fast players to play best. It comes as no surprise therefore that to play a complete attacking and counter-attacking game one needs to have all 15 players plus reserves practising intensively together. There is no point having the pack off scrummaging for an hour while the backs try to amuse themselves and invent new moves. Moves don't make a pattern of play.

Our squad had to utilise their short periods of time together to the full. We spent hours practising in simulated match conditions until running, supporting and scoring tries became second nature and not the second option. Kicking has always been the first option in any Irish team I played on and subsequently watched. Happily, the Ireland v. Scotland game in the 1991 season reversed that trend.

We changed all that. We told the media and the public what we intended to do. The players committed themselves to playing this type of game and my responsibility to them was to remove the fear of making mistakes or of trying and not succeeding. Our philosophy was simple: 'If you're not making mistakes you are not trying hard enough.' To eliminate mistakes and to perfect the individual and combined unit skills and passages of play, the team needs to practise a lot together and certainly not in instalments. Practice itself does not make perfect: only perfect practice makes perfect and perfect practice needs time, concentration, patience and a total lack of fear of making a bollox of things. Dick Greenwood the English coach, was honest when he said 'You can't give a whole nation a brain transplant' or words to that effect. He was responding to the question: 'How or what do you think of Mick Doyle's philosophy of running attacking rugby?' His response was honest and expected. He was saying that one needed to change an awful lot of minds from negative to positive thinking.

Rugby journalists who have not played the game at the higher levels have no in-depth understanding of how the mind of a top-class football achiever works. They cannot appreciate the vast difference between subtly negative attitudes and positive ones. I don't blame them for that: all they lack is experience. Where I do take issue with the media, however, is their apparent willingness, oft times rejoicing, to embrace the negatives — the fear of being wrong, and not going boldly for the positives. And when their fears are proven correct they feel justified in gleefully going for the team's jugular.

I'm sure I made lots of mistakes. I know I took a lot of the high profile pressure and the flak away from the players for obvious reasons. Cud, Fitzie and I impressed on the players the positive things we were doing and thinking and we kept negatives away from them. They knew that no matter what we said in public the only thing that counted was what we discussed privately, in our own group.

If you want to fail there are seven ways to ensure that you'll be a failure quickly.

1. Expect to fail
2. Have no goals
3. Have no plan

Lynne and I on our wedding day.

This photograph was taken in the summer of 1982, when things were unravelling for Lynne and me.

Barr-na-Coille, near Johnstown, Co. Kildare where Lynne and I lived until 1982.

The Cud and I, 1984.

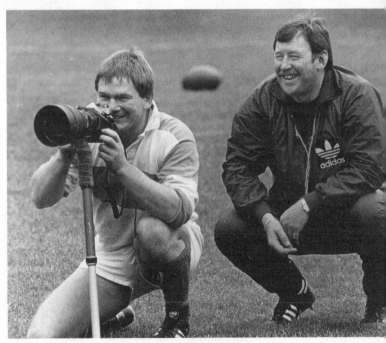

Fitzie and I,

The sash my father didn't wear.

ie, J.R. and myself at the Phoenix Park, 1986.

Young ladies growing up. Amanda (left) and Sharon Doyle, 1988.

More than just a hound dog: 'Rambles' in 1988.

WANTED

Mick 'Dangerous' Doyle in connection with a number of
daring international raids and the theft of the Triple Crown.
The above picture was taken in 1968, before the operation,
when Doyle was asked to pull a few flankers for the Lions
in South Africa.

Footnote: Approach this man with the utmost caution.
Beware the beguiling smile and Irish blarney. For assistance,
contact any member of the R.U.W.C. — specialists in
dealing with such cases and whose advice costs as little as
a quote or a pint.

*The front and back pages of the invitation
card for the Rugby Union Writers' Club
Annual Dinner of 1986, at which I was
presented with the Pat Marshall
Memorial award. I thus became the only
person to hold that award and the Rupert
Cherry Prize in the same year.*

THE RUGBY UNION WRITERS' CLUB
Founded 1960 (26th year)

25th Annual Dinner
and Presentation of the
Pat Marshall Award

LONDON, 27 FEBRUARY, 1986

Mandy on our wedding day, 11 March 1989.

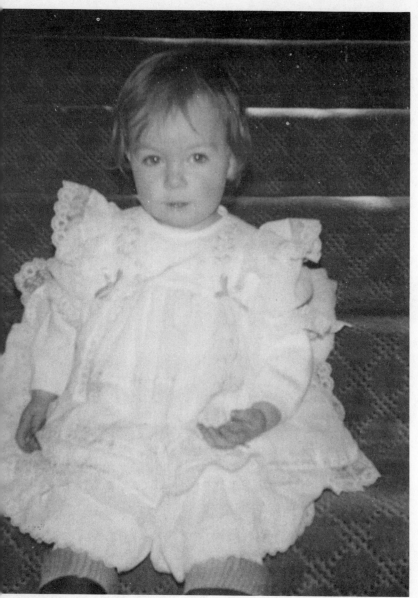

…a, May 1991, aged 20 months.

Mandy and Emma with the Doyle menagerie, 1990.

Four Doyle women: Mandy, Emma, Sharon and Ama

4. Mix with negative people

5. Always criticise

6. Have no opinions of your own

7. Always procrastinate — never put off 'till tomorrow what will do the day after

There was no way that we would expose our young players to that. They had their dreams and I for one, was going to make damn sure that they at least had the right to express their dreams in tangible fashion. We heightened their individual levels of self-esteem and gave them the right and the responsibility to 'go for it'. My philosophy is and was: If you think it, do it — don't mess about, just do it. It is the responsibility of the other players to support you and their responsibility if it doesn't come off. Nobody will be blamed for trying — never, ever!

So very quickly the ethic became quite clear — if you see a chance go for it. In other words, 'give it a lash!'

Giving it a lash does not mean stupid mindless throwing the ball around with no purpose. What it does presuppose and depend on is having your defences well-covered, your fall-back positions rehearsed and knowing that you have the correct base from which to attack.

'Give it a lash' is a horse-racing expression which I got from a veterinary colleague and flat mate of mine from college days, one Gerald K. Barry who was an amateur jockey among other accomplishments. It simply implies that when the final shakedown occurs and the winning post is beckoning, the crowd roaring and everything happening in milli-seconds about you, you give the horse a nudge of the riding crop and you go for it. That's what makes Lester Pigott, Tommy Carberry, Jonjo O'Neill, Pat Eddery, Tommy Stack, Liam Ward, Dessie Hughes, Michael Kinnane, Tom Taaffe — need I go on — different from the rest. When the opportunity is there for a split second you must be ready for it, recognise it and go for it. Give it a lash!

If you hang about waiting for your opportunity to present itself you are lost. It is incomprehensible to me how many scribes and others in print either misunderstand or misinterpret that simple philosophy and attribute to me a mindless egotistical urge to ask players to commit suicide for me! (In fact we had a superb move called 'suicide' which Ralph Keyes did in Japan with Brenny Mullin and John Hewitt — and we scored as well!)

Anyone who knows me from my time with UCD, Leinster, Blackrock and Ireland knows that I believe in exact detailed preparation before any game; that I never dwell for too long on the opposition's strengths other than to enumerate, understand and respect them. But I do dwell at length on what we are going to do from set piece positions and what we are free to create from any position.

You cannot tell a team to play 15 men attacking rugby one minute and ask them not to make mistakes on the other hand. It's like saying 'take your time and hurry up about it.' Attacking rugby does not always mean running rugby. It may do mostly, but all good rugby teams can kick well either for better position or to get themselves out of trouble. We were not good at the latter because Deano was not in the Ollie Campbell or Tony Ward mould, as a defensive kicker.

What I decided to do with the players' help and the selectors' support was to develop the game we were best at — attacking pressure rugby, not the boring, clinical crap that is passed off as thinking or professional coaches' rugby. You know their philosophy: 'Oh, that's alright in practice, but how does it measure up in theory?'

Anyway, on to the 1985 Championship and Triple Crown or the Criple Trown as my father outlaw, Victor Henry Thompson calls it.

In January 1985 England refused to play us in the snow. No they didn't. The game was called off on the Saturday morning because the terraces were dangerous due to heavy snow on Friday. All the players and selectors adjourned to Donoghue's Pub and had the best preparation for the season we could have had — a genuine Irish piss-up with sandwiches and soup as 'soakage'. It built up a grand spirit and camaraderie among the whole group and it was time well-spent. We beat the living bejaysus out of England about ten times during the course of that afternoon, as well as Scotland, Wales and France for good measure. We had New Zealand on their knees by the time we were ejected.

Next we travelled to Scotland. Cliff Morgan (Bective, Cardiff, Wales, The Lions and BBC) sent me his video of *Wales — The Crowning Years*, covering ten years in the late sixties and early seventies of some of the most superlative rugby ever seen in these islands. Trevor Ringland played that Welsh video incessantly and made everyone watch it. It really showed how a team endowed with geniune talent in key positions could develop self-belief and play the most superbly effective football. It also showed Barry John's genius allied to his quite incredible work rate, Gerald Davies' brilliant running and scoring feats, the importance of quick possession, the 'arrogance' of J.P.R. Williams and the whole team's fantastic support of play. It is a classic rugby video. Dewi Griffith (also BBC) sent me Harry Carpenter's *Great Sporting Occasions* to keep the players' minds fresh. I think the Mayo Gaelic football team still have it.

We watched those two videos a lot that weekend in Edinburgh. Edinburgh was cold, wet, windy and it was snowing! Ideal weather for running with the ball! We had our dress rehearsal in Dublin before we left and had enunciated and articulated our strategy and tactics in attacking and defence. We had reckoned on about 40% possession of the ball from 'set pieces' and intended to run at Scotland at every chance we got: Scotland play their rugby at a fast, furious pace. Our team could 'up' the pace even more and we decided to maintain a furious tempo. The Scots were sceptical. We did no training on Friday — a 15 minute game of Mickey Mouse touch rugby to stretch the limbs and occupy the minds, much to Joe Gallagher's approval. We spent the afternoon at a tenpin bowling alley while The Cud operated a kid's aeroplane: he couldn't get into it so he wrapped himself around it. Morale was high. I went to meet many of my old mates at Edinburgh Wanderers' new clubhouse and spent a pleasant hour chatting and reminiscing. I met my team at the movies, by prior arrangement. Of course, as normally happens in Scotland, the Scottish team were at the same cinema. I suppose great minds do think alike! Hugo MacNeill was our cinema buff. They must have had theirs as well — probably John Beattie; hardly 'The Bear' (Ian Milne).

The team and supporters were in good mood at the North British Hotel — a watering hole I have always liked. Two years previously in 1983, while I was a lowly sub-selector, Ann Orr, Phil's wife, had spent the Friday night in my room with me! It happened like so. There is considerable juggling around of rooms at international weekends to cater for rugby wives, girlfriends, love, sex, making babies, avoiding babies or whatever. The girls stay away from the lads on Thursday and Friday nights usually, and meet up with them after the game on Saturday. It worked like clockwork especially when Philly Orr was organising it. This particular weekend Harry Booker and Philly decided that my single room was too small for me and would I mind moving into a much nicer double room. I agreed of course. Philly explained that Ann couldn't get a room and would I mind if she shared with me. Did I mind? I was deloired! I think my alacrity sort of worried him — I wasn't supposed to display such enthusiasm.

Anyway Ann and myself, after a superb dinner with some of the alickadoes and Mary Brophy as well, adjourned to the lounge where we all had a few nightcaps. Nobody knew the sleeping arrangements, except for the four people mentioned.

I went off to get the key and returned to the group addressing Ann directly and suggesting that it was time for bed; she obediently left the group and demurely followed me out of the lounge and into the lift. I wished I had a video to record the sheer incredility on everyone's face. Doyler — the cad!

We half expected that Philly might have physically divided the room and barricaded my bed into a corner. Of course everything was normal and having worked out our nocturnal and early morning itinerary Ann and I slept the sleep of the just and in separate beds. We looked well at early morning coffee robed in our off-white Shelbourne Hotel dressing gowns. It was a memorable weekend — a lot of buzz about Ann Orr sleeping with Mick Doyle, the bastard, and Ireland beating Scotland. In 1985 I had an early morning breakfast in the North British Hotel with some journalists from BBC NI. The breakfast and the chat was broadcast by the BBC, a novel experience. Bill McLaren even produced his boiled sweets to share with us.

After a quiet lunch the team and myself went out to rehearse a few line outs, calls and positions in the garden beside the hotel. I had promised the lads a fine day and lo and behold the wind and rain stopped. I was assuming God-like proportions to suit the occasion. We had a short team talk — I remember telling them that I had tremendous admiration for them as men and as rugby players and I knew that they would give a good account of themselves.

We had to tear Trevor Ringland and Keith Crossan away from the Welsh rugby video to get them on the bus to the ground. At the hotel door I met Gerald Davies in the flesh. He had heard about our Welsh video and asked me what we learned from it. I replied, 'Gerald bach, we learned that if fifteen fucking thick Welshmen could play rugby like that so could 15 Irish men.' I was half joking.

Gerald and I are mates since the Lions rugby tour in 1968 to South Africa — a grand little trip. He is a special person to me and one of the best wing three-quarters of all time. He is an altogether lovely man. He is now a respected journalist and ham movie actor.

We started and finished the game like a hurricane. I could have shot Hugo twice in the first ten minutes for making a bollox of two scores. Scotland were ahead 18–15 or so towards the end but I was delighted at our team performance. If we lost playing like this, so what? But the character of that team, especially of its captain, Ciaran Fitzgerald, wouldn't concede anything 'till the final whistle. Before going down for the final scrum of the game Fitzie said to the backs, 'This is the last ball lads, make it count.' Brian Spillane broke left off the scrum, drew about four Scots, we won the ruck and there followed the most exquisitely-timed passing, receiving, and running I have seen from an Irish team. Trevor Ringland scored in the corner and Mick Kiernan converted. This formula was to be repeated often during the next few years. Ciaran driving his men, their response and Michael Kiernan's winning the matches.

We had won by playing fifteen-man attacking rugby and I was never more proud in my life. It was close; we could have been beaten, possibly should have been, but indomitable spirit, self-belief and trust in their own instincts saw them through and all the practice, practice and more practice we had put in had paid off.

The thinking, the response and the execution of the play that culminated in that try had become second nature. The delicate finger-tip passing and timing was instinctive but Paul Dean was the playmaker on that and many more occasions.

I will never forget that first game nor Fitzie's team talk beforehand. The Scots, as always, took it well and we had a good night up to ten o'clock — I don't remember any more about it till the bus left the next morning. I remember enough.

Our next assignment was against Wales in Cardiff. They kept telling us that Ireland hadn't won a game there in eighteen years, since 1967. I kept reminding the Welsh journalists that I was on that 1967 winning side and that this 1985 team was a totally different proposition to anything Wales had experienced before from Ireland.

We had no fear of being beaten and if we were it would take a better team to win. We were going to attack them all day and see what happened. On Friday evening we took the team into Cardiff to walk on the pitch and let the boys feel the atmosphere.

We arrived at the ground 90 minutes before kick-off on Saturday and resolved to do the business. While Fitzie was out tossing the coin Phil Orr and Donal Lenihan kept reminding everyone of the task in hand and fired them with a will to win. Cud was on the door keeping all the well-intentioned well-wishers out and away from the players. With about six minutes to go to kick off Cud arrived into the room in a panic. 'The feckin' Welsh,' said he, 'want us to line up facing the committee box stand and they're going to sing their ould songs at us.' 'No sweat', says Ciaran, 'we'll line up and sing back at them.'

Out on the pitch they lined up, linked arms and defiantly sang back at the crowd. There was to be no intimidation with this team — no bloody way. We hurled defiance at them all afternoon and with a combination of superb play by our team, especially Nigel Carr, Philip Matthews, and Brian Spillane, perfect orchestration by Bradley and Dean, the pinpoint accuracy of Mick Kiernan's boot and six missed penalties by the unfortunate Mark Wyatt, we recorded an historic win.

The Irish supporters were great and *Molly Malone* rang out all over the ground in the last quarter — even the Welsh crowd were singing it. It was a magic day. The eighteen years of subservience in Cardiff were truly exorcised.

During the dinner I was called from the table to take a call from the President of Ireland! It was Colm Costello and Dickie Roche phoning up to offer congratulations. They had tried in vain and had to invoke Paddy Hillery's name to get through.

My Dad had flown in from Spain for the game so I was whisked to his room for a quick drink and well wishes all round. Des Douglas, John Hickey and John O'Shea were there and Clive Rowlands joined us for a jar. As an aside Clive said to me, 'Mick, are you available to coach the Lions to South Africa next year?' I said 'I'm yer man.' He then said, 'I'm available to manage the tour: we'll have a great set-up.' I agreed. I'll tell you more of that anon.

Back in Porthcawl the celebrations were in full swing at our hotel. Porthcawl caters for the newly-weds and the nearly deads and since I was neither it fell to Karl Johnson and Sean Diffley to put me to bed or something like that. I was at peace with the world. Our young team had proven what they were made of and the 'brain transplant' to which Dick Greenwood referred was obviously not being rejected. England stood between us and the Triple Crown. But first La France!

To prepare for the encounter with France Cud and myself flew to Paris to observe the France v. Scotland game. I arrived at Dublin airport with no passport. Cud was almost in tears and his tie was in ribbons from twisting it. However Aer Lingus sorted me out and we got there and back without mishap. We also learned nothing except that France were tough and mean, and I mean mean.

A fortnight later, the French came to Lansdowne Road. It was a brutal game and we were lucky that it was a draw. France were lucky that our team was composed of quiet young sportsmen. Up in the stands watching them I couldn't help thinking back to a similar game twenty years earlier. I wished we had that particular 1965 pack out against this 1985

French pack. I can assure you that Ray McLoughlin, Ken Kennedy, Sean McHale, Wigs Mulcahy, Willie John McBride, Noel Murphy, Ronnie Lamont and Mick Doyle would have put manners on this particularly sneaky lot and beaten them out of Lansdowne Road.

That is no reflection on the 1985 team. They were not that kind of pack! Just as well! Michael Kiernan's five penalty kicks drew the game for us.

Brian Spillane had eight stitches inserted into his gaping lower lip and Philip Matthews had a nasty, almost crippling shoulder injury. Luckily they both recovered for the Triple Crown match against England.

The lead-up to that final game is almost a blur now. However I remember the salient, unforgettable things about it. We tried in vain to get the players to regard it as just another game but we gave up and said 'It is our Triple Crown and nobody is going to deny us!' We steeled our minds to go for broke and prepared as we did for every other game. The build-up was like a countdown to a wedding day and none of us could bear the wait.

On the Thursday before the match, I had a date to keep. I had agreed months earlier to be 'talked' into addressing the Publicity Club of Ireland in Jury's Hotel on my chosen topic which was simply 'Up the Media'. Bill Tyndall (now deceased unfortunately) and Bill Ambrose (Business and Finance) kept me to my word. It was quite a day.

I was allowed the licence to do and say whatever I liked about the media and it was a pleasant send-up. A few people took it seriously but that was their problem. Ned Van Esbeck didn't turn up. Colm Smith did an interview in the bar afterwards but I don't remember it — it read very well all the same. Smithy was always good at filling in.

I did an interview with ITV out at Glencairn Stud in Leopardstown and nearly got trampled on by a couple of frisky fillies. The interviewer asked me if it was true that our chairman, The Cud, had sold quite a valuable racehorse. I replied that it was not true and that the horse hadn't been fed and had walked out on him. Everyone who knew Il Cuddio knocked a great kick out of that. The horse was Drumlargan but was referred to as Drumgargling by some punters.

At last the great day arrived — perfect weather, perfect pitch and no wind. We made our plans accordingly. We were intent on giving our home crowd the best value for money they ever got. At about twenty minutes to kick off The Cud entered the dressing-room and told us that it was pissing rain. Sixteen voices, mine included said 'Fuck it anyway!'

The game is sketchy to me — I remember Brendan Mullin's try which was answered by Rory Underwood in the second half. I remember that the 'nerves' set in and we didn't play very well. I can see the Pony Express banner proclaiming 'Dr Doyle's Transplant Clinic' on the East Stand but I can remember above and beyond all that, Ciaran Fitzgerald's incredible spirit and indefatigable leadership. At ten points all with minutes remaining the occasion demanded and the players required that spark of inspiration and Fitzie was the man.

It is well-recorded that he asked his players the single question: 'Where's your fucking pride?' There was no way he or they were about to settle for a ten-all draw — no way on earth. He threw a long, unsignalled ball to Brian Spillane who soared skywards to reach it. Philly Orr and Donal Lenihan had reacted like true champions and followed the flight path of the ball. Mick Bradley trailed behind awaiting his cue. 'Spillers' pots it into Philly's hands, he drives on, feeds to Mannix (Lenihan) who takes on the English forwards; the ruck forms, ball on the deck, in the twinkling of an eye Brad has the ball in Mick Kiernan's hands and as Deano applauds Mick drops his goal and we had won 13–10. Irish rugby pride had been restored with a vengeance.

Dick Greenwood was as gracious and generous as I knew he would be. He complimented the team and reckoned I wasn't a bad brain surgeon.

Life is a funny thing, you know. Way back in 1965 I replaced Dick Greenwood as open side flanker on the Cambridge team when he had qualified as a teacher. In 1966 Martin Green replaced me as flanker and in 1986 he replaced Dick Greenwood as England coach: funny set of coincidences. Michael Carroll, a true friend and a gentleman to boot, sent me to bed in Mandy's care early that night.

Before the game was long over I was giving the Jameson and Guinness a 'bit of a lash' myself and had a hard time keeping a straight face during a BBC interview with Bill Beaumount. The reception at BBC's headquarters was poor so Bill had to repeat the question four times. I gave the same answer three times and while Bill was trying to sort out the problem I turned to Fitzie and observed: 'If I repeat that answer once more I'll start to believe it meself.' I didn't know it but John O'Brien had kept RTE's cameras rolling all the time so I was caught in the act.

And so a historic year had finished. We had won our Triple Crown Championship and almost beaten Australia. I am enormously proud of that team and its achievements. I admire every player in the squad that year. I am eternally grateful to Michael Carroll for his support as President of the IRFU and to The Cud for being himself, also to the selectors for their support and advice.

Above all I pay the major tribute to Ciaran Fitzgerald my friend and captain. Without Fitzie it would not have happened.

In the end the pride, the passion, the commitment, the responsibility and sense of self-worth that Fitzie and his players expressed so nobly in 1985 laid many ghosts and myths. They proved to all and sundry that they could not only produce the goods when the chips were down, but produce them in style.

We gave it a lash and we were proud of it.

12

The Phantom Tour

'I don't mind any player spending the night before a game in bed with a girl. What really bothers me is the guy who stays out all night looking for one.' (M. G. DOYLE — ADAPTED FROM A QUOTE BY AN AMERICAN FOOTBALL COACH)

AT the beginning of the 1986 season I was asked if I was available as coach to take a Lions team to South Africa around June 1986. I replied in the affirmative and it was confirmed that Clive Rowlands would be the manager. I was advised, as expected, not to publicise the fact but to let the Four Home Unions secretariat advise the media and the public when the time came to do so. As is also usual, it became common knowledge long before it became official. How often I wished I could come face to face with the leader of the 'Leakers' Union' in the flesh. He would be leaking more by the time I'd finished with him, especially from places from where it would be quite painful to leak!

As the home international season wore on, the predictable, well-orchestrated cacophony emanated from anti-apartheid groups. Pressure was being exerted on anyone remotely connected with the tour or on anyone who might conceivably be associated with it.

I gave many interviews airing my opinions of sport and sporting links with any country and dealing specifically with my views on apartheid.

Apartheid in South Africa, like the Irish-style apartheid we saw practised in Northern Ireland for over fifty years, and

146

the apartheid we practise in the Republic of Ireland when we assign second-class citizenship to some of our people, especially travellers who want to settle, is a vexing and complex question. It is a lot more confused than you would think from listening to the people who make the most noise on the subject.

Apartheid is the Afrikaans word to describe 'separate development' and was introduced by South Africa's National Party on their accession to power in 1948. However, the apartheid mentality had its origins long before Britain handed over power to the white electorate in 1910. I would refer keen students of the topic to *Apartheid — A History* written by Brian Lapping in association with Granada Television for a full account of the development of this odious system.

I experienced, from a distance, the obviously visible 'separateness' between whites and non-whites during our Lions tour in 1968 and learned enough about the subject to realise what a complex problem it was. It was not all black and white, to coin a phrase. South Africa in 1968 had an unsettling effect on me as had Romania in 1979. Strange how there were never similar crowds on the streets moaning about Ceaucescu. We could visit him as often as we pleased. He was game ball as far as the selective moralists were concerned. All peoples yearn to be free to make their own choices, live where they wish, marry whom they wish and vote for their own nominee on an equal basis with everyone else.

If the question were all one-sided, however, it would be somewhat easier to address, but white South Africans, like the Israelis and Northern Irish Unionists, have their own equally valid point of view. They fear being swamped in a free-for-all and have felt, tragically, that they could only defend their interests at everyone else's expense. Thus apartheid, a system which was not only cruel but stupid as well. Happily, its days are now numbered as the more enlightened whites, under the courageous leadership of President de Klerk, have finally rejected it.

The world community rightly condemned apartheid, but there is hardly any country in that community which can put its collective hand over its heart and say 'We're clean.' The anti-apartheid movement has a democratic right to call for sanctions against South Africa if it wishes. It has a right and a responsibility to acquaint governments of breaches of human rights and abuses of human dignity that occur in any country. However, in exercising its rights in a democratic society it does not have the right to behave in a manner that is tantamount to denying the citizens of that country their own rights, particularly freedom of choice.

It is farcical and totally unacceptable to me as a free Irishman to be told that in order to grant civil rights to non-whites in South Africa I must be denied my right to travel there, to trade there or to play any sport there! It is totally ridiculous. My sport is rugby: it is the only major sport in this country that has united people on this island — Catholic, Protestant, Jew and otherwise for over 100 years. It has not caused divisions among Irishmen and women: on the contrary, it has given them a common purpose. All my experiences of rugby in this country or anywhere else for that matter is that it unites people. Anyway, it is a simple matter of principle. Even if I am totally wrong and misguided, I still claim the right, as a free citizen of a free country, to travel wherever I choose whenever I choose. To compromise that right is, in effect, to make me a criminal. In addition, it leads to crazy anomalies brought on by attacks of selective morality.

For instance, when the Irish government threatened not only to withdraw its monetary support for Irish rugby but to threaten to withdraw passports from potential rugby tourists in 1980 (did I say this was a free country?) it cheerfully sent the Irish Olympic squad away to Moscow — the last imperialist capital — with every blessing! And this just months after the Russian invasion of Afghanistan!

I detest apartheid as I detest any system that consigns any human being to second-class citizenship or to circumstances that are beneath human dignity. It exists everywhere but the poor bloody South Africans at least had the guts to acknowledge it openly and to give it a name: apartheid. The Afrikaaners may be many things but at least they aren't hypocrites.

I make no defence of such systems of government. Nor am I a passive supporter, and it is beneath contempt to imply that people with views like mine are either racist ourselves or supporters of a racist regime. I hate apartheid. But that does not affect my right to decide for myself what my personal response should be.

Anyway, during the 1986 season the four home unions panicked and the tour to South Africa was called off. It was a shame. However, as it was the centenary of the International Rugby Board two major games were arranged: The Lions v. The Rest of the World in Cardiff on 16 April and The Lions plus France (Five Nations) v. The Rest on 20 April in Twickenham.

The Lions assembled under manager Rowlands and myself as coach in the Angel Hotel in Cardiff on Saturday 12 April. John Rutherford, Ian Paxton and John Jeffrey phoned me to say they would be delayed until Sunday and arrived in time for the first training session together — or just about. It's a long drive from the Borders to Cardiff and I admired them for taking full part in the session.

The Rest team, including France, also stayed at the Angel under the benevolent regime of Bob Templeton of Brisbane (manager) and New Zealand's Brian Lochore (coach).

Obviously there was fairly regular fraternisation between all the players and Templeton, Lochore, Rowlands and Doyle observed a regular routine of a drink and a chat before dinner.

Our Lions group quickly developed into a very happy harmonious outfit and one could sense the regret and loss of not being allowed to tour South Africa. This became more acute when it became common knowledge that a New Zealand Cavaliers team had accepted the invitation to tour there and play Test matches.

Our Lions group mixed very well in Cardiff and we all dreamed about what might have been. Colin Deans was a good captain, but totally different to Fitzie. Obviously Scottish coaches, like Jim Telfer and Derek Grant imposed themselves more on the players than we in Ireland do and I found that Deano expected me to be talking more than I did; equally I had expected him to be running the show more as captain. However, it was merely a question of degree. We got on well.

Fitzie and I had developed a partnership and shared responsibilities more than is the norm. We often reversed roles, particularly in running some of the talking, discussion and training sessions. It helps to break the monotony and develops teamwork of a more democratic nature. That is not to say that Scottish coaches and captains are wrong — far from it! They have taught all of us a lesson or two in the recent past. I have no doubt that Colin and myself would have developed a good partnership on a tour. I have equally no doubt that our Lions group would have given a good account of itself on the full tour and would have been an extremely happy, lively team.

In the game itself injuries early on to John Rutherford and Wade Dooley, two key players, made our task more difficult against the World XV and we were just beaten in the end.

Our team room in the hotel was at one end of a blocked-off corridor — but it did the job. Clive Rowlands and all the players and myself plus Tudor Jones our trainer/physio and Barry Michaels, our secretary, retired to our team room after the official dinner and sang to our hearts' content. The Scottish boys told us that they had more laughs, and sang more in a couple of days in Cardiff than on the whole Lions Tour to New Zealand in 1983. I believed them. Colin Deans was a very central character to the Scots. I like and admire him but I disagree totally with his views about Ciaran Fitzgerald which were expressed in his book *So You're a Hooker Then*. These views do him no credit.

Later on in the night of the game in Cardiff Clive and I slipped away to an Indian Restaurant and amid Keema Nan, Tandoori Murgh, Bhuna Ghosht and Prawns Bhuna we picked the Five Nations team (including France) to play against the 'Rest' on Saturday 20 April.

The following morning at Cardiff Arms Park the French joined us and Clive read out the team. It included Jean Condom (or the 'other French second row' as Fred Cogley used to call him), Laurent Rodriguez at wing forward and Serge Blanco at full back.

Little Jacques Fouroux, *le pauvre petit*, nearly did his nut — he wanted the whole French contingent involved but we were having none of it. As it was a two match 'tour' we had decided to give all the Lions players a game which was the only sensible, fair and democratic thing to do.

When we'd cooled *le petit general* down he asked me; 'Meek, I suppose you wish me to coach *les reserves?*' I said, 'No Jacques, you'll look after the backs.' He was overjoyed and nearly kissed me. He soon got over his shock about selection and the discovery that Rowlands and Doyle were not going to capitulate.

His handling of the back line in training was tremendous and he introduced a few subtle moves which were brilliant. Serge Blanco is not alone the best full back I have ever seen he is also probably the most talented footballer I have ever witnessed. His skills are consummate and his instincts electric. He is good fun as well.

We travelled by coach from Cardiff to London — the first and probably the last ever Lions Tour of England and Wales!

After training in London we had to attend a press reception at Twickenham. Afterwards there was the obligatory press conference. Somebody suggested to me that I didn't see eye to eye with Jacques Fouroux (or yer man Farouk as Cud called him). I replied that it was difficult to see eye to eye with a bloke who was only four foot six. That settled that, I thought. Another question: 'Do you have a language barrier with Fouroux?' 'No,' I said, 'his fucking language is just as bad as mine.'

We had an interpreter along with us to help with the French. I delivered an impassioned talk (at least I thought it was) after training on Friday morning — as impassioned and forceful as one can be when you have to stop in mid sentence while the interpreter translated it (minus the fucks and bolloxes) for the French. Blanco was in tears laughing, Condom looked totally bewildered and Rowlands kept coughing into his handkerchief. Donal Lenihan who was captain of the Five Nations team let the occasional snigger out of him. The interpreter and myself finished 'neck and neck'. Some said he just pipped me and at the end of it most of the French were wondering what was up with me!

Rowlands' team talk the following day before the match was even funnier. He delivered half of his in French, broken Welsh and pidgin English. He kept insisting that the lads play from *le coeur* (the heart) while pointing to his head. They all thought he was mad.

On the Friday night when I thought I had the lads safely tucked up in bed Mandy, who had just arrived from Ireland, and I went out for a meal to Veronica Shaw's restaurant. As we were finishing a superb meal and were becoming all lovey-dovey, Veronica asked if we would join Chris de Burgh for a drink at his table. Chris was in the middle of recording his *Lady in Red* album and was having a night off with his manager. I later realised that he is an avid rugby supporter and a passionate Irish one.

We enjoyed a few hours of ribald jokes — what else would you expect from the author of *Patricia the Stripper* — and copious bottles of champagne. We left in the wee hours and got back to our hotel, the 'lovey dovey' having progressed to 'red roaring randy' at this stage and we both (Mandy and myself, not Chris and myself) gave vent to a performance of amorous acrobatics, something like Rod Stewart's *Midnight Trampoline*.

I didn't realise that Jeff Whitefoot and The Shark Jeffrey were rooming on either side of us until I joined the lads for Rowlands' team talk the next day. The Shark relayed verbatim every word, nuance and inflection of Mandy's and my voice heard during our midnight sexercises — enormously embarrassing but at the same time quite satisfying to be the subject of such conjecture and obvious adulation.

Some of the lads had wondered if I was capable of such loving heroics and suggested perhaps that it may have been a blue movie or a record that I had been playing. The old joke about spark plugs and jump leads also got an airing!

Ian Milne (The Bear) and Dessie had a deal going. The Bear was playing against a giant prop called Floppy Van der something or other. Dessie had agreed that if The Bear signalled to our box in the stand that he was in trouble then Dessie would come on and relieve his burden. In due course The Bear began his frantic signalling and Dessie returned the compliment with a two-fingered salutation. It was hilarious.

We were well-beaten in that game but as Clive said afterwards it did not reflect our true strength.

Kevin Murphy, the English team's physio, had replaced Tudor Jones for our Twickenham encounter. That night after dinner he unscrewed the brass piping around the bar counter, reassembled it, filled it full of Guinness and drank the bloody lot. I can still see his face.

We were all saying our goodbyes and all the best players from all over the world were congregated in the hotel bar, making promises to meet and write at later stages. Rory Underwood told me he wanted to do something in my honour. He was a teetotaller then, a Coke man, but he drank a half pint of Guinness 'just for you Mick'. I was very touched but just got out of the way as he ran for the loo to get it back up. I appreciated the gesture, truly.

My abiding memory when we were all about to leave for home was of Clive Rowlands in charge of about forty fully pumped-up signed rugby balls for clubs at home in Wales, standing outside the hotel and wondering how he was going to get them and himself home to Wales without a car! I can still see Barry Michael rolling around laughing.

That week was an incredible experience. It is indelibly imprinted on my brain, as is an earlier week I had spent in the company of New Zealand's J.J. Stewart in Cardiff during the Welsh Centenary Year — one week of a supposed rugby seminar! But that will have to wait for another day. J.J., John West, the referee and myself established the 'Emerging National Choir' which represented every country in the world except Wales.

I regretted enormously that we didn't tour South Africa. I feel sad that at a crucial time in early 1986, talented young amateur players from Scotland, England, Wales and Ireland had been denied their sporting ambition of playing against the best rugby-playing country in the world.

13
World Cup 1987

'Life is what happens to you when you're making plans'
(JOHN LENNON, HUMAN BEING, SINGER/SONGWRITER,
FAVOURITE BEATLE)

THE fourth Saturday of April 1987 dawned beautifully warm — perfect for our first official World Cup squad training session at Wanderers RFC's picturesque Merrion Road grounds. As I motored up from my home in Sherlockstown, Co. Kildare my mind was turning over the myriad of plans, options and wonderful anticipations that rugby's first ever World Cup generated.

I was looking forward to meeting Syd, Michael Molloy, Joe Doran and all the lads again after a fairly successful home international season. We had disposed of England 17 points to nil in positive fashion to avenge the scrummaging insults of the previous year in frozen Twickenham; we had won well in Cardiff for the second successive time in the 1980s by two goals to a try (10–4); we had almost beaten France in Lansdowne and certainly deserved to after an incredible first half performance; and we had succumbed to Scotland in Edinburgh in a game we could have won but which we never got really into. I won't bore you with any further detailed analysis except to comment briefly on the Wales and England games.

We dominated England from the kick-off. For days beforehand we were being taunted incessantly and reminded of our scrummaging problems of the previous year. I had done a fairly detailed personal 'true life' interview with Gay Byrne on his radio show and even Gaybo had inquired about England, scrums and other such trivia. I assured him and his listeners that we would have our day on Saturday — and we surely did.

Marcus Rose, yet again, was cast in the role of Richard, *Coeur de Lion* and his Merrie Bande of Crusaders. He was a good full back but did not measure up to the predictable accolades that the English rugby media heap so fulsomely on selected, poor innocent players from time to time. Poor ould Marcus was Fleet Street's current pin-up boy. We thought that he was accomplished and brave but slow and we intended to make him run a lot and try to isolate him.

In drizzling rain we won a lot of possession and attacked with high kicks from Paul Dean and Mick Kiernan that were inch perfect in height, length and direction. Nigel Carr caught Rose with one tremendous jack hammer of a tackle under a high ball which shook him like the impact of an Irish pothole. His gum shield escaped and headed for the end line, his legs wobbled and he appeared to be concussed.

He was replaced by a player of lesser class. Dr Mick Molloy said that Rose was not concussed. His eyes couldn't focus because Nigel's tackle had dislodged his contact lenses: the English team medic thought otherwise and foolishly substituted him.

Naturally we didn't complain. With the departure of lion-hearted Marcus we dominated totally in every facet including scrums and we were happy: so were our loyal supporters. That night Willie Anderson, playing his bagpipes, led us around the dungeons in Fitzpatrick's magnificent Killiney Castle Hotel and Chris Crowley of Galwegians slow-danced an old time waltz with me.

We beat Wales in Cardiff in our last game of the Five Nations' championship and proved our worth. I had been personally chided by one journalist for having lost the confidence and support of my players because I had told them the hard facts of rugby life in a private meeting in the Royal Marine the week after the Scottish game. The journalist got his story wrong. The players reacted as I thought they would and expressed their support for me by word and deed, none more so than our captain Donal Lenihan who behaved as a captain should.

I have been telling my players in private what I thought of them, as rugby players, without frills, for as long as I have been coaching. Players like and respond to honesty and react positively to constructive healthy criticism once they understand and trust the source.

My many friends in the Welsh rugby media were annoyed that this piece had had an airing in a Welsh newspaper also and went out of their way to allow me the opportunity to refute whatever I wished. I told them the facts and assured them that they were free to ask any member of the Irish squad for their opinion.

After the game we were jubilant and as Eddie Coleman (chairman), Donal Lenihan and myself were combing our hair and adjusting our profiles in preparation for the press conference I was seized by a group of team heavies and thrown into a hot bath in my clothes. As I surfaced I heard Dessie Fitzgerald remark: 'We fucked you into the bath Doyler to show you that we don't like you and have lost all confidence in you.'

I enjoyed a few quiet pints with Derek Quinnell and Tony Gray (coach) after the dinner that night and looked forward to our historic meeting in Wellington, New Zealand on 25 May 1987. All these happy memories were in my mind that April morning on the drive up to the World Cup squad training session.

As I arrived at Wanderers' Club House I met Keith Crossan who told me that there had been some trouble at the Border, near Newry on the way down from Belfast earlier that morning and some of the boys had been delayed — Nigel Carr, David Irwin and Philip Rainey who had been travelling together. Shortly after that Davy Irwin phoned and told me about the awful bomb blast that had devastated poor Judge Gibson and his wife and nearly killed my three players.

David was driving, Nigel the front passenger and 'Chipper' was in the back. Major parts of the debris had hit their car. Nigel was badly injured, Chipper was badly shaken but uninjured and David was as cool and as calm as a breeze as we spoke. He had pulled his two companions from the total wreck that had been their car only seconds earlier and helped get them to Daisy Hill Hospital in Newry, about five miles away.

David is an iron man with an inner steel to him that his soft Ulster brogue and his open, broad smile camouflage very well. His instinctive reactions, allied to his skills as a doctor had a major bearing on the health and safety of his two friends that day.

The Ulster players phoned home to assure their parents, wives and girlfriends that they were safe and well. It is no exaggeration to say that if any of these young Irishmen and their team mates, whom I was proud to manage and coach, had been able to meet any of the cowardly perpetrators of this sheer, wanton, brutal, pointless act face to face, they would not have lived to gloat or boast about it in the sick circles from whence they emanate.

I will repeat, rugby on this island has managed to do what no politician or churchman or other sport has succeeded in doing — unite the hearts and minds of people in all parts of Ireland. In fact, rugby has provided this framework of positive involvement often despite the protests and actions of various political groupings, legal or illegal, legitimate or illegitimate.

I am a Catholic, Kerry-born Irish nationalist and I'm proud of it. I don't have to ram it down anybody's throat and I certainly do not have to kill, bomb or maim anyone to prove it.

I accept a temporary, *de jure* political and trade border between both parts of Ireland — not an ideological one and certainly not a border dividing minds. I do not doubt that this island will be united peaceably at some time. That is my own personal viewpoint. I think as much of a Ballymena man as I do of a Ballybunion man and I respect the traditions, cultures and differing allegiances of people from all parts of Ireland.

Irish rugby, I might add, is also representative of some of the most extreme viewpoints of all shades on this island — but it unites us and will not divide us. I believe that most people involved in Irish rugby share these views. The players certainly do. It was devastating for them to hear of what happened to their three mates.

David and Chipper joined us later but Nigel's career was in ruins: one of the most dedicated Irish players in Irish rugby was cut down in his absolute prime. It was a tragedy for him and an irreplaceable loss for us. I went to see him in hospital the following Tuesday accompanied by Ken Ging. He was glad to be alive but looked like a man of 80 years of age. Only his enormous fitness saved him from more crippling if not fatal injuries. He wrote a personal letter to every member of the team before we left for New Zealand and it was a sad group that left Ireland without him.

We assembled in Dublin on Tuesday 12 May and left Ireland on Wednesday the 13th. We stayed at The Copthorne Hotel near Gatwick Airport and left for New Zealand on Thursday the 14th accompanied by the Welsh party, our opponents in the first game. It was a long boring, energy-sapping flight and some thirty-six hours later we checked into our hotel in Auckland.

It was then that my ould heart decided to teach me a lesson. After a couple of memorable days of tender loving care in Auckland's coronary care unit I joined the team who had gone ahead to Wellington. I was touched and tearful at the welcome the lads gave me and the care, help and attention which Syd Millar, Mick Molloy and Joe Doran lavished on me. At this stage I was taking all sorts of tablets and was scared to go to bed at night on my own, without two sleeping tablets. I swam in the hotel pool in Wellington under Joe Doran's beady eye. I found most things bewildering and didn't enjoy anything really.

New Zealand is a lovely country and its people are warm and friendly, if a bit straitlaced — totally the opposite to the Aussies who couldn't give a 4XXXX about anything.

Syd did much of the team preparations and Donal Lenihan had to take more control on himself. I was functioning at about 50% both mentally and physically and have no doubt now that I should have come home of my own volition or have been sent somewhere away from rugby. Either way it was almost an impossible task for all of us, Syd, Mick Molloy and myself, to make the correct decision for many obvious reasons. Hindsight is a great teacher! It was, after all, my team — I had started off with them back in 1984 and I didn't want to let them down. But they may have been better off without me at that time.

However I struggled on, on two cylinders for most of the time and did the best I could. My problem was mental of course — when your daily rations are supplemented with various blood pressure, heart and stress regulatory tablets accompanied by those little white pills to ensure non-wakefulness during the night, I found that I became disorientated after a while and hugely dependent on Mick, Syd and Joe. I had become a patient and ceased almost to think for myself.

My greatest fear became fear itself and my greatest enemy was being alone at night. I craved for Mandy to be with me so that I could hold on to her and allow myself to be mothered by her.

Our team's performances against Wales, Canada and Tonga were in no way reflective of our worth and we knew it. I believe we got our pride back in the second half against Australia although they beat us fairly well.

Our World Cup was a litany of injuries. Harry Harbison couldn't play in any game due to a serious back injury and retired from rugby. Consequently, a very raw but brave Terry Kingston had to learn a lot in the space of a few days before his first cap for Ireland. John McDonald came out as Harry's replacement. Paul Dean received a severe bruising on his ribs three days before the Welsh match and Derek McGrath was playing his first international game for about three years. Philip Matthews was stamped on viciously in the first ruck against Wales and was almost immobile for the rest of the campaign.

John McDonald damaged himself against Canada so we had to send for Stevie Smith from Ballymena — the player that Syd and I had wanted as second string to Harry Harbison in the first instance but couldn't get! It is hard to believe that the manager and assistant manager of an international team, only one of whom was a selector (me), could not have the one player we specifically requested. We were also told that Willie Sexton who hadn't played for months, would get fit during the World Cup campaign and should be selected ahead of Derek McGrath. We won that vote but only by three to two.

The injury situation reached the point where I received a telex from Billy Tyndall and the Naas/Kilcullen Lions Club offering the services of the 'Tow' Haydon and Eddie O'Loughlin with full CVs for both 'players' which I reproduce here for posterity.

'Mr Mick Doyle,
Irish Rugby Coach,
Bushcutters Bay Hotel,
Sydney,
Australia.
6th June, 1987.
As requested, Naas/Kilcullen Lions Club is delighted to furnish you with background information on two of its members. We understand they are under consideration for selection and we wish them well.

Anthony Oliver Longhaul Haydon (otherwise known as 'Tow')

Sex

Twice in Lawlor's carpark and once after a donkey derby at Kilteel.

Occupation

TV Star

Early signs of greatness

Kicked an old lady outside Croke Park in 1956 and ran. From the age of three he blew his nose with his left hand.

Outstanding Achievements

Exposed himself in Dreamland Ballroom to 1,500 screaming Dickie Rock fans. Exposed himself in Naas, Carlow, Bodenstown and Longford golf clubs. Finished in fifth place in Feis Ceoil 'Tell the Time' competition. The winner, a Zambian, was closest by getting the day correct.

Sporting Achievements

Paid into Clonmel Dog Track on two occasions. Going it alone he finished sixth in the Eadestown sports three-legged race.

Best Position

About five inches to the left.

Ambition

To eat a raw chicken through a comb.

Greatest Regret

Scoring in Bangkok.

Edward 'Maktoom' Begobs O'Loughlin

Sex

Never. Results of tests expected in ten days.

Occupation

Professional cow spotter. He also has cattle for sale without spots.

Early signs of greatness

Wore his sister's dress to Tow's stag party — Tow wore it home.

Outstanding achievements

Was awarded the Patsy Lawlor Peace Award for reporting a fight at a sale of work in Straffan Town Hall.

Sporting Achievements

Captained the Kill under 18's when he was 23. Returned a hurling ball from the crowd in Thurles in the 1960 football final.

He still owns the plastic bag that his first rugby boots were bought in. Scored twice at Dunlavin ICA'S Dinner Dance.

Best Position

Over a bit.

Ambition

To one day play with the wind.

Greatest Regret

Not bringing a cap to Leopardstown on Stephen's day.

And Mick, even if you decide not to play them we wish you the best of luck on Sunday.

Naas/Kilcullen Lions Club.'

Injuries were bad enough, but even before a ball was kicked in the first game against Wales, there was the very worst kind of fiasco. People at home were stunned to observe our team in Wellington standing to attention to the strains of James Last's orchestra playing an emasculated, popped-up version of *The Rose of Tralee*. At the same time we were treated to a near replica of the Cardiff Arms Park crowd singing the Welsh national anthem. It was a superb recording: closing ones eyes and first listening to it was nearly enough to transport one back to Cardiff and its partisan Welsh crowd. We took a lot of blame and abuse for that but it was not our decision; it was decided by the Irish Rugby Football Union. We even had a telex message from HQ to ensure that we wouldn't be tempted to play the Irish national anthem!

The players were extremely perturbed, annoyed and let down by that stupid decision. Certain elements in the IRFU committee had obviously decided that flags and anthems would be to the forefront in the World Cup — like in the soccer counterpart or the Olympic games. It was argued by this faction that since the Irish team represents two geographic and politically distinct entities — two 'different administrations' were the words used — it would be wrong to play *The Soldiers Song* at any World Cup function. This ridiculous viewpoint prevailed despite the fact that the anthem is played at Lansdowne Road at every game and is played before every game in every country in which Ireland played rugby — Japan, South Africa, New Zealand, Australia, Argentina and so on. I understood that some of the Ulster players who were named to me would not stand for it. I know now that this was not correct.

In fact the Ulster players were the most vociferous of all in Wellington when Syd had to announce that the anthem wouldn't be played. At a meeting in Syd's room with Donal Lenihan and me, which was attended by Sir Ewart Bell, President of the IRFU who was in New Zealand not as a member of our party but as a guest of the World Cup committee, a strong delegation of players let it be known that they were insulted by not being allowed to play the anthem which to them was part and parcel of Irish rugby.

One Ulster player, with passion in his eyes, reminded all present that to him, as a Protestant Ulsterman, Irish rugby meant a green jersey, green shamrock, Lansdowne Road and *Amhrán na bhFiann* — nothing less!

The IRFU were adamant. A decision could not be changed without a full committee meeting — the usual platitudinous excuses. The players then insisted that they must have something to stand to in representing Ireland as well as for all the people at home, and poor old Syd spent two or three hours scouting around Wellington for something appropriate and Irish. The only tape he could find was James Last's version of *The Rose of Tralee* and this was played.

The players were badly let down. We were all so hurt. It made us the oddities in world rugby — typical Paddy amateurs. It is an insult to decent Irish boys to subject them to that a long way from home. Connie Houlihan, my long time friend and journalist extraordinaire who has an instant grasp of those kind of situations, suggested to me the following day that he was surprised the IRFU hadn't insisted that we play God Save The Rose of Tralee. That's called hitting the nail on the head.

Canada then sportingly agreed not to play their anthem either. Syd can be very persuasive! Hans de Goode (or de Baddie as he is affectionately known), the Canadian captain, was gracious in defeat at the post-match press conference but bemoaned the fact that they couldn't use their anthem specially since most of them had just about learned all the words of it.

Tonga came next and mercifully their anthem tape got lost!

Finally against Australia in Sydney our anthem again wasn't played but everybody stood while Moss Keane and his merry band of touring supporters, aided by a goodly number in the crowd, sang *Amhrán na bhFiann* and our honour was maintained.

It was a sorry demeaning episode in Irish rugby history. hope the guiding powers are not allowed to get away with i for the 1991 World Cup whenever Ireland plays away from home during the competition. It makes me see red when think of it. I feel the point should be emphasised that if one accepts or calls for the principles of majority rule in one part of this island, then it should logically follow that the majority view should rule when it comes to our national anthem for the Irish rugby team.

Pat Spillane, that incredible Kerry Gaelic footballer, was truly amazed when he heard *The Rose* being played on TV from Wellington. 'Christ, Mick,' he said, '*The Rose* would never motivate me to go out and beat the hide off anyone. It would just make me soft and nostalgic .' He was right of course — and *The Rose of Tralee* is after all Kerry's own anthem.

I told Ned Van Esbeck at the end of the World Cup, before we left for home, when he inquired why Tony Ward wasn' selected against Australia, that the reason was that he didn' know all the words of *The Rose of Tralee*! It saved a lot o argumentative banter.

We never did ourselves justice in that World Cup for man reasons. I'm sure my ill-timed mishap was the cause of much of our problems.

England did tremendously well against Australia and migh well have won. Scotland and France acquitted themselve really well and Wales redeemed themselves against Australia.

The draw was stacked in favour of Australia and New Zealand for the final. However France put paid to that and kept our side of the world up and then Wales finished of Australia.

It was sad for that superb Australian team but they hadn' played well during the cup and the wheel began to come of in the second half against us. New Zealand were far and away the best team — they were awesome in their power and scoring potential, and made very, very few mistakes.

We left Sydney feeling quite sad — it had been hectic and rushed and we really didn't have time to meet many people or see anything of Australia and New Zealand.

Our liaison people in both countries couldn't have been better and things were relatively well-organised for a first World Cup effort. I have no doubt but that the World Cup is here to stay and will become a big event. From an objective point of view the 1990 soccer World Cup in Italy, apart from Ireland's performances was, for me cynical and boring. World Cup rugby has an awful lot more excitement and depth to offer and I feel that we are at the start of a major explosion in the game.

I arrived home disorientated and shattered during the second week of June — I had been away from home for about a month. The girls met us at the airport. And my, how we were thronged by representatives of the IRFU! Precisely two people turned up to welcome us home — Paddy Moss, the IRFU secretary, and Paddy Madigan. I was grateful to them. Richard Bourke, an old school mate and a true friend, invited me down to the placid calming womb of Parknasilla where he was then manager. Tom, Sonny and Jackie my old friends made Mandy and me welcome home. We spent a lovely therapeutic fortnight there walking and swimming and fishing with Gerry Casey.

I drove home with Mandy on Sunday 28 June to a business that was in chaos and to three months of sheer mental agony. I was still taking the prescribed tablets and was afraid not to take them. I resent or rather resist being a patient or feeling like a patient. I prefer to be in charge of my own positive health and to make my own decisions about my health with proper medical advice, of course. Dr Mick Molloy was very supportive during this time and had had a long conversation with Dr Norman Sharp, the superb cardiologist in Auckland. He would not have released me from intensive care to anybody else in the world except Mick Molloy. Mick and I had been colleagues on the Irish team for many years and we knew each other well — he knew me better than most. It was lucky for me that he did.

Early in July I was trying to relax, avoid stress and at the same time to preserve and resurrect the remnants of my business. Unfortunately, the business had gone into reverse during the years I was coaching Ireland. It started to nosedive when I came home from New Zealand and now it was basically just Lynne and myself again trying to piece the business jigsaw back together. Meanwhile, Mandy was doing her best to get me to reduce my stress level! I must be unique in having a former wife and a fiancée to look after me. I was a lucky man indeed and I will always be in debt to both of them.

A number of good friends gave me a lot of help when I most needed it. They would, I know, prefer to remain anonymous but they know who they are. Andy Butler will.

The extreme stress, the fear of a recurrence of my 'coronary incident' whatever it was, and the effect of the tablets I was taking eventually impacted adversely on me. My mind and body started to go out of synchrony. I would wake up in the morning after a tablet-induced sleep and get ready for the day's work. By lunchtime I rarely knew who I was, what I was saying or doing. Depression and total lack of confidence ruled most afternoons.

Mercifully Mandy took over, cancelled my work schedule, sent me to bed, took me off all tablets and treated me with love, warmth and understanding together with a one week grape diet, numerous herbs and probiotic lactobacillus capsules. She detoxified me for over one week and altered my life. I owe her my sanity and my life.

Another therapeutic weekend as John Fahey's guest at his fabulous Limerick Inn hotel helped my recovery immeasurably. In the end I was glad to be finished with coaching and selecting. I know that I gave everything I had of me to it and many things that I could not afford. The stress induced by the twin requirements of almost giving 100% each to coaching Ireland and trying to keep a business going and carve a living was unreal. I am surprised I lasted out as long as I did. I am quite a strong and resourceful person but in the end I had to admit that I could not live life in the outside lane any longer. I think the fact that I loved all those players so much and wanted to give them every scrap of me that was worthwhile kept me going.

I know that I would do it all again but with quite a few changes. I know that financially I could not afford to do it unless somebody was picking up the tab. It is not financially possible to look after all the interests of a national team properly for three years *and* earn a living as well. It cost me an awful, awful lot of money.

On the other hand, it gave me some of the most incredibly satisfying things in my life. It brought me in contact with gifted, intelligent, talented young players and many great people in the world whom I have always admired. It gave me the chance to dream the dream, aim for the stars and give it a lash. It made me humble in victory and philosophical in defeat. It shaped my life and the public's perception of me for the rest of my life.

It gave me the confidence to assess and trust my own instincts and to rely on people. It made me unselfish but sometimes, of necessity, ruthless. It gave me a short but lovely three year span in which to state to anybody who wanted to listen that performance is king and if the performances are paramount the results will follow. When we played well we generally won.

It allowed me the licence and the freedom to help players to unshackle their minds and shake off imposed constraints, to recognise their own strengths and weaknesses and to strive for the ultimate expression. If they had never won a match I would be enormously proud of all of them. Coaching and looking after them for three years was far better and far more important to me than the twenty caps I won for Ireland as a player.

Very few men are ever fortunate enough to be entrusted with the honour and the task of looking after the well-being of an elite squad of international players. I was privileged to have met two great squads in my coaching career — Leinster and Ireland. I am proud of what I did and what we achieved. We feared nobody and gave of our best. I said at the beginning of my tenure with Ireland 'Do not judge us by results alone, rather look at and understand what we are trying to do.' I do not have much patience with some rugby critics. They have an utterly negative view of the game and they somehow manage to transplant their negatives into the minds of intelligent, gifted players. Dick Greenwood was probably right when he said: 'You can't give a whole nation a brain transplant.' But I didn't need to transplant any brains — my guys had brains to burn all along and I just implanted the seeds of freedom among a few cells — their own neurones did the rest.

I would love to have coached Wales or France — they have had an abundance of class players but they have been sacrificed at the altar of coaching. Coaching must be in the service of players, not the reverse. Ciaran Fitzgerald has now embarked on his term as Irish coach. I am delighted for him and I wish him and his players well. I expect him to be a great coach and I know Ireland will hold its head up with pride among the top nations of the world again and be counted. In the 1990–91 season just past his Irish team has recaptured the spirit of 1985 and the Green Jersey is being worn again with pride.

My son Andrew is enjoying serious rugby with Lansdowne and I spend much of my leisure time watching his career and offering advice when I'm asked.

The *Sunday Independent* indulges me by giving me my own weekly column which keeps me involved in a stress-free way, in the game and out of mischief most of the time. When one tries to write an honest, objective, informed column it is difficult to avoid certain controversy at times and quite often I suffer pangs when I am required, in the interests of objectivity, to be less than complimentary to people who are involved in the game — players, selectors or others — people whom I like and admire a lot. However, there is too much that is not being said and such omissions are selective and dishonest.

However, I do miss the close, personal contact and the camaraderie that existed in my coaching days. I miss most of all the quickening of the pulse, the huge buzz, the roar of the crowd and the enormous surging eye-brimming avalanche of emotion, admiration and pride that hit me every time *my* team took the field.

They were something else.

'Those were the days my friends/We thought they'd never end . . .' Amen.

14

Lynne, Mandy & Me

'Everyone says they'll marry till death, and they're divorced a few weeks later. I've lied to the judge twice myself.'
(MUHAMMAD ALI)

FOR some people separation, the legal variety, represents a limbo from which they can never escape. For others it is a purgatory in which they suffer for a time before being released to freedom or what passes for freedom in an overwhelmingly Catholic Church dominated country like Ireland. For Roman Catholics who have contracted an unsuccessful marriage in Ireland there is no legal way out except for the limbo of separation. Officially divorce does not exist, without doubt a denial of a basic human right for all citizens and a stain on our country's character. I find it insulting as an Irishman to be told that some day we may have divorce because if we perhaps removed the obstacles to legal divorce, the Unionists might change their minds and think we're great people and they'd be queuing up to join us. Indeed? There is no sympathy for the hundreds of thousands of people who are contracted into miserable marriages and who should not be forced to remain in them: rather do we see the cynical expediency of exploiting the political gain line. Every time the subject of divorce is brought to the surface by some reasonable, caring politician he is jumped on the by the generals of the Catholic clergy and their vociferous storm troops.

The Irish Catholic Church has always preached more negatives than anything else — a plethora of 'thou shalt

172

nots' predominate most teaching. This male celibate body has no idea, despite its assertions to the contrary, of the mental agony people go through who are trapped in hell on earth.

I deplore the way in which even the little discussion that divorce receives is wilfully distorted. Knowing it to be untrue, anti-divorce fanatics tell us that if divorce is allowed for 50,000 or 100,000 people in Southern Ireland then Irish Catholic marriages will all fall apart and everyone will want to be divorced. There must be an awful lot of shaky, Catholic marriages about!

What utter rubbish! Nobody, least of all the proponents of fair-minded, realistic, long-overdue divorce legislation, is forcing divorce on anyone; nobody is being pressurised into divorce. All that is being asked is that divorce be available as a civil and human right to people who in good faith married one another years earlier, but discovered later, basic incompatibilities that prevent them from remaining together any longer as man and wife. Marriage is basically a civil ceremony and the marriage contract is a civil contract.

Lynne and I married each other in a civil ceremony in Bristol in 1966 and the marriage was sacramentalised by the clergy of the Catholic Church in the Pro-Cathedral. We appreciated at the time the pomp, ceremony and solemnity.

We were legally separated in 1983 in Ireland and we were divorced by a civil 'decree absolute' in Bristol in 1988. We were lucky. Quite a number of friends and acquaintances have had to resort to ending their marriages through foreign divorces and remarrying outside the state.

This is a sad sorry state of affairs and reflects badly on our country. Of course if your mentality is such that you can perform mental back-somersaults which link contraception, divorce and abortion together then nothing any reasonably-minded person could say will make any difference.

If Catholic priests were married men with families and responsibilities and experienced all the pressures and strains themselves I have no doubt that divorce would be on the statute books already — you can bet it would.You could also wager that divorce would be the norm if women clergy were ordained. Women have far more maturity.

It is interesting also to reflect on the significant number of priests who, in good faith took their vows of chastity and the rest and pledged themselves to Christ and the Church *forever*, find that they can no longer subscribe to these vows or remain priests and are allowed their 'freedom'. Not so the poor Catholic laity who find themselves in parallel circumstances. Such duplicity is a distortion of human values and a cynical reminder of a long-gone hierarchy.

Equally mind boggling and mystifying is the practice of Church annulment. The whole question is a ludicrous exercise in semantics.

As I said I was one of the lucky ones but it was an unbelievably hard, lonely road to embark on, particularly in a small country like Ireland where one is known to a great many people. However I have nothing to complain about at all personally so I am not writing this out of bitterness. I was very fortunate that I had a lot of friends and the love and respect in every shape and form of two fine women, Mandy and Lynne, as well as my children and close family.

When Lynne and I legally separated Mandy had not entered the picture. It was basically Lynne and myself coming to our own joint decision with advice from our friend and solicitor Brian McLoughlin and support especially from my father and a few important friends.

Ray McLoughlin's confirmatory advice of placing the children, Lynne and myself in that order in the hierarchy of concern was comforting and supporting as was Ned Thornton's consistent contact. The major priorities for me were that the children were looked after properly and that Lynne and I worked hard to remain good parents and develop another type of relationship other than a married one. The typical Paddy-like, male, macho, umbraged attitude did not occur to me and would have been totally unhelpful in our situation.

When Andrew was starting out as a boarder in Blackrock's Willow Park School, Lynne and myself took him there for his interview and his first day in school. Sharon and Amanda were attending national school in Kill and when their time came to go boarding at Alexandra College we met Ms Eithne Ryan, the principal, and explained our separate but intertwined circumstances to her. It was important that the schools' staff knew this and to their credit they both responded really well and took good care of our children.

We visited them often, sometimes separately, sometimes together, and one or other of us collected them on Friday evenings or Sunday mornings in Andrew's case, and brought them back to school on Sunday nights. As often as possible we all had lunch together on Sundays, usually in Barr-na-Coille, sometimes in Pinewood Lodge in Blessington. It was important for them that we were normal parents in every way except for not sharing our personal lives any more.

Lynne was enjoying her relationship with Bill Tyndall at this time and I was either on my own or in and out of a relationship with Maria. Towards the latter part of their secondary school life I had been introduced to Mandy by Sharon and Amanda.

Since I was the motivator or fulcrum for all this activity I had to develop and maintain a very open mind and not allow things that might normally aggravate me to bother me. Billy was accepted as one of the family and after a while I had jettisoned my understandable resentment of him living in my home and being there when my children went to bed or got up in the morning or needed cuddling or playing.

If you have never experienced marriage or a close male/female relationship and the joys of children, I suppose that living alone can be very satisfactory. However, if you have, like me, lived for 17 years of marriage and dreamed dreams together with your beloved and brought three lovely children into the world, then it is devastating to have to face the cold reality of living on your own. You can surround yourself with all the paraphernalia of modern living and all the audio-visual extravaganzas; you can locate yourself in the most beautiful setting and indulge your senses in the most up-to-date, fulfilling leisure activities but all that cannot even begin to measure up to one moist little good-night kiss with sticky little fingers wrapped around your neck or a little body creeping into your side of the bed at night for warmth and reassurance. It cannot compensate for the lack of physical and mental love from a partner nor the kiss and cuddle as soon as you step inside the door when you come home from a weary day. A nice house cannot kiss you good morning or cook your breakfast and send you out to meet the world with a smile of encouragement.

Living alone means that there is no 'your side' of the bed; you don't need to 'bag' a chair; it's always your turn to put out the milk bottles, order the coal or wash the dishes. There is nobody to share anything with. The whole damned house is yours and everything in it but it means little or nothing. The numbing emptiness shrieks at you.

Nothing can compensate for not being around when your little children cut their fingers or your son wants to play football with you or tell you how he did at school.

Damn those people who have no sensitivity or comprehension of how devastating separation is for two young people for whom things have gone wrong and who are looking for a chance of finding their peace, self-respect and the pursuit of the happiness to which they are entitled.

The proposition that people marry in haste and separate in haste is pure uninformed bullshit. Very few people want to jump into separation and divorce on a whim or because they have had their first disagreement. The monetary cost alone is daunting enough: adding the other factors turns it into a nightmare.

There are many people, unlike Lynne and me, who are forced to endure the nightmare of a broken, violent, degrading marriage; they seek the help of their leaders and advisors for a merciful escape only to have the door slammed in their faces. The only recourse for many is mentally to leave the Church and live with a new partner in an Irish limbo. The Church doesn't seem to care for, and obviously does not deserve these decent people whom it consistently alienates. Life cries out for less Irish Catholicism and more, much more Christianity.

Lynne and I have retained a deep respect for each other and a love that is almost brotherly and sisterly. With common sense and a common purpose uppermost in our minds, we resolved our differences and tried to help each other to keep on developing as human beings capable of forming a loving relationship with some other person.

Lynne had made her mind up that Billy was the right man for her. I didn't agree and told her so. However, it was her choice and I respected that choice. I met Billy over a few drinks on our own in the Osta John Devoy in Johnstown and discussed their relationship and my attitude to it. I don't think Billy fully realised how much I supported Lynne in her decision. I told him that I had brought her over to Ireland in 1967 and *felt* responsible for her, and always would.

I said that I was happy for her that she felt that she could find happiness with him. I said that I expected him to look after her well-being and to respect her and the interests of my children. I told him that if he messed her about I would kill him, metaphorically speaking of course. He knew what I meant. Billy was a decent bloke, intelligent, good-humoured and easy to get on with. He was in charge of advertising with the Irish Press Group and was very good at it. He had an enormous number of acquaintances and many good friends.

He was always the life and soul of any gathering and could sing very well. He was hilarious company.

The first time I met him was at Templeogue Tennis Club. I was 'subbing' for Niall O'Neill on the County Kildare Club second team and a guy called Bill Tyndall was to be my partner. I didn't know him and Niall described him to me as being tall, skinny, browny red hair with a fag in his mouth and a few bracelets hanging out of each wrist.

I waited for him for about half an hour and started a 'knock up' with a guy who seemed to be waiting for his partner also. After about twenty minutes of 'good shot', 'sorry I nearly hit you' and the like I asked him whom he was partnering. 'You, you fucking eejit' came the reply.

We lost the games, drank the opposition under the counter and told stories till 2.30 in the morning. Billy headed for Leeson Street, and I headed home to Barr-na-Coille.

I met him a lot over the next few years and he was very helpful to us in our business — advertising, marketing and the like. Lynne formed a ready attachment to him which was genuine and round about 1981 it flared up into a full-scale love affair.

Initially when Lynne and I separated and I left home to live on my own in Naas, things seemed quite strange to a lot of people. Lynne and I had appeared to be such a well-matched, loving couple that they couldn't believe it and thought this new affair was a mad fling that would soon pass. Lynne and I had discussed it and I knew what she wanted and that she was single-minded enough to go after what she wanted. Like most women she was far more incisive than a man in that situation.

At any rate, Billy and Lynne were getting quite a lot of stick and felt that many ill-judged remarks were coming their way from people who should have known better. I must say that I was annoyed for them, Lynne particularly, and accompanied the two of them to various watering holes in Naas —

Lawlor's, Fletcher's, the Ivy Inn and the Manor Inn, basically to express solidarity and to convey to all and sundry that if anybody was to be upset or put out by Lynne and Billy's relationship it surely should have been me and since by my presence I was making an obvious statement of assent to the relationship there was no earthly reason for any further hassle in this regard. Everybody got the message and the questioning looks stopped.

I chose to live on my own most of the time even though I was in a developing relationship with Maria. But my children's well-being came first and since they were inextricably linked with Lynne she was obviously high in my priorities also. My old friends as well as our joint friends were equally querysome and the major problem I had with them was to stop them taking sides. Unfortunately, human nature seems to zero in on tragedy, turmoil or impending trouble.

Many of my drinking mates in Lawlor's, for example, would often involve me in discussions about Lynne, Billy and myself. These were guys who came out every night without their wives for a few pints and like many a man anywhere in the world, attempted to sort out the world and his aunt over a few beers. I've done it myself and enjoy it still but it becomes a bit tedious after a while.

The facts were simple. Lynne and I had discussed the whole subject with our children and explained fully to them that we both loved them, that we ourselves were disagreeing too much and couldn't live together anymore and that we would have new partners in our lives. We reassured them that both of us would continue to love, cherish and look after them and that we would both be spending as much time as possible together with them. And we did all those things.

For me, it was a very tough time mentally, although I kept up an outward bonhomie. I found it difficult to come to my office each morning located in the same grounds as the house and find Billy's car in the drive.

I had agreed to provide a home for Lynne and the children and I knew it was best that she should stay in the family home and have her boyfriend there as well. It would have been totally 'thick' and wrong to have had it any other way despite the multifarious advice I received to the contrary. Some nights when I was hitting the gargle fairly heavily I found myself in the drive of my old home by sheer accident. My subconscious mind obviously had strong attachments.

My father, many cousins and close friends had been very supportive of Lynne and me in our traumatic times of separation and trying to build our lives again. I think both Lynne and myself keenly felt the awful loss of Auntie Mai at that time for no doubt she would have been an enormous help to both of us without bias or favour. Lynne's Mum and Dad were obviously upset but supportive. They are still among my best friends and have accepted life as it is now and are very important to me.

My own mother had died tragically in a drowning accident in 1962 in the River Maine at the back of our garden in Castleisland. She had been throwing dead flowers into the river without realising that the banks had been cleaned and the river dredged. She lost her footing and we found her three days later in Castlemaine Bay. She was obviously a terrible loss to Tom, Dad and me as well as to all our family: more to Dad than anyone else, naturally. She was a warm, lovely, serene woman who never raised her voice in anger in her life. She and Dad loved each other with a quiet intensity and a tenderness that was a model for Tom and me.

I didn't really get to know her well until I started to come home for holidays from Newbridge College. I had been living at Riverside in Currow until I was thirteen-years-old and was then sent boarding to Newbridge. I always regarded Currow as my home and still do, funnily enough. I spent half my holidays initially with my grandmother, Momma Dennehy and the other half at home with Mammy, Daddy and Tom. As I moved into the teenage phase of my life and was becoming aware of girls I found that I could talk to Mammy and learn how to get on with girls. I remember once when I was about seventeen and heading for the flesh-pots of Ballybunion and Matt Sullivan's Central Ballroom accompanied by Billy Browne, Micheál Brosnan, and Noel Browne, I asked my mother pointedly, 'What do you do with girls?'

She was embarrassed and said: 'Micheál darling, you'll dis-cover that soon enough for yourself. You're going to meet all kinds of girls in your life, but take my advice and do not go out with any girl that you wouldn't be proud to bring home with you.' It was sound advice and I knew what she meant.

I have missed Mammy on so many occasions in my life since her death. She never knew either Lynne or our children. They have missed a lot, not knowing her. Likewise she would have adored Mandy and little Emma and would have recognised in Mandy an almost mirror image of her-self: her gentle voice, her peaceful bearing, her serenity and her lively personality oozing with warmth. I hope we all meet in the right place some day when our time comes.

I missed my mother when Lynne and I separated and kept saying to myself: 'What would Mammy do in this and that situation?' Even in death she has guided me.

I didn't involve friends in my private life at the time for many reasons. I didn't want them taking sides and I didn't want incessant discussion which only prolongs the agony and makes a bad situation worse. When you are the recipient of unwanted and unsolicited advice you could begin to slide into a self-pitying, self-justifying routine and allow yourself to become polarised and painted into a corner — the wrong corner.

I kept my own counsel and a few people who really know me assured me that I was doing the right thing. I myself felt that I was doing the right thing — albeit unconventional.

Lynne and I were partners in our businesses at the time. One or two failed but we have maintained a business together throughout all the most difficult period of both our lives and are just about getting things together now and are still partners.

Through all this time Lynne had gone through her own traumas in trying to adjust to a dying relationship with me and develop a new one with Billy, while looking after the children and running a business.

She is a remarkably strong-willed woman, with a single-minded, purposeful way of going about things. She does not express emotion much whereas I'm the exact opposite so it is no wonder we got out of synchrony so often.

Lynne was a strong, supportive business partner in our most difficult time after the separation. She worked hard to ensure that everything was done and done properly. Without her strength and tenacity everything would have been far more difficult than it was. She also got on well with Maria after a few hairy moments at the beginning and I even think they exchanged viewpoints about me now and again!

With the arrival of Mandy into my life, my whole mental process changed and I was able to look at things with a more balanced view. Mandy gave me the love and affection and support which I had craved and this impacted positively on everything else I did — particularly taking up the Irish coaching job.

While I was coaching Ireland, Lynne valiantly tried to run the business while I was away a lot — both physically and mentally. She did a wonderful job and it is to her credit that we have a developing business together today.

Mandy and Lynne fitted in well together from the start — Lynne had known her for quite a while before I did, but not very well. She was bemused at the thought of 'Mick and Mandy' and threw in the odd 'baby snatcher' crack in good fun. Mandy has never interfered with the business side of my life although she is a shareholder and partner in Mick Doyle Marketing International Ltd. Lynne does not interfere in our life together and was supportive of us both from the beginning of our relationship.

In February 1987, before we played England, I did a deeply personal interview with Gay Byrne recounting what had happened to Lynne, Mandy and myself. Gay was a very intelligent, sensitive interviewer and he helped me to publicly unburden quite a few bits of unwanted mental baggage. Everybody seemed to have heard it and their positive response was astonishing to me. It was very therapeutic for all of us involved.

Lynne has had some hard times herself over the past number of years. Billy became terminally ill and died in 1989. She was, naturally, very upset for she loved him deeply. Our children were also very fond of him and mourned his death.

I personally developed a great liking for Billy Tyndall. He was a good man. He climbed many mountains himself in his short, eventful life and lived life to the full. He had built up a great professional reputation and a good developing business at the time of his untimely death. I was sad and honoured to walk behind his coffin as were the thousands of friends who paid their last respects to him.

I'll never forget the humour in the depths of sadness as the cortege rounded the corner at Poplar Square in Naas to the church. A policeman stood to attention and saluted the coffin. Larry Cooke, his brother-in-law, and John Greely saw the instant irony and one of them remarked: 'Bejaysus, it must have been the first time in his life that Tyndall wasn't trying to duck a Garda.'

His sisters Edna, Larry Cooke's wife, and Eta were devoted to him and missed him tremendously. I met them one evening as they were going into Lawlor's Hotel for a drink and told them I would join them after I did some shopping. Edna wasn't feeling well and Eta took her home. I never met her for that drink: she died shortly afterwards. She was broken-hearted. She was his twin.

I was honoured to attend a private lunch in Lawlor's in early September 1990 hosted by Shay Hyland, Bill McHugh and other friends of Billy's from the Publicity Club of Ireland. They presented Eta and Lynne with a commemorative plaque to Billy. It was a nice gesture and we all reminisced about him. Lynne and Eta appreciated it particularly and now the pain and grief for them has turned into happy memories of hilarious times.

Lynne is now putting her own life back together again. She has been a great mother to our kids and has been a good friend and partner to me. I love her now as I would the sister I never had. Over the years we have come a long way and done a lot of things together. We have brought three beautiful, wonderful children into the world and they have all been a joy and a blessing to us. We are both intensely proud of them and without going on about it we are proud of their achievements. They are all thankfully well-balanced children with well-developed, informed minds of their own. Our separation does not appear to have been a problem for them and I have no doubt that our closeness, respect and fondness for each other helped in a major way. Also the fact that with Maria and her family we formed one big group from time to time helped to reduce the by-products of sep-aration. Mandy fitted into the extended family as though she had always been there. She understood completely that I had commitments and responsibilities which had to be honoured consistently and to the fullest extent.

Lynne organised the services of her solicitor in Bristol and she and I again decided on our divorce arrangements without rancour, remorse or dispute. It is a very final thing, divorce, but after the separation it was a formality. There was no big 'Hallelujah Chorus' when we received our decree absolute, just a pride that we had achieved it and still remained strong friends. Lynne and I helped each other to grow up into better people than we were when we started out together. I am proud of the manner in which we faced up to our problems and responsibilities, avoided blaming each other at any time — and I mean any time — and got on with the positive things of our lives.

We have come a long way from that Wolfhounds tour of Bristol in 1963. Of course I wish that we never had to separate or divorce, but turning back the clock is a waste of time and I know now that we made the correct decision in 1982.

It led me to Mandy and a love, peace and tranquillity I never knew I would find. It also helped me to help create another little bundle of joy and energy called Emma Louise Doyle. I hope she turns out like her mother.

15

Mandy, Marriage and Emma

'A wise man is a man who knows enough to realise how little he knows'
(MARGARET MEREDITH, SCHOOLTEACHER — CURROW 1952)

I LOOKED at the quiet, smiling, handsome woman across the desk from me. It was about 11.00 o'clock on a wet Tuesday morning in February 1989 and I asked her if she would marry me. She looked me straight in the eye and said something like: 'That wouldn't be a proposal would it?' Regretfully I answered no as I was already spoken for. She was Amy McAleer, Registrar of Omagh District, Co. Tyrone, Northern Ireland and I was trying to arrange that Mandy and I could get married in the Omagh Registry Office the following March. Ms McAleer discussed the arrangements and requirements in detail and facilitated my planning with grace and charm.

I had fulfilled the residential requirements, was in possession of a 'decree absolute' from Bristol, and was of sound mind and limb apart from a Hugh Gibson-induced hangover. My prospective bride, Amanda Power-Smith, spinster, of Westown, Johnstown, Naas, Co. Kildare was unfettered and free to marry me. She had to have the necessary forms completed by the County Registrar in Naas and Amy McAleer reserved the date for us — Saturday 11 March 1989.

We were expecting Emma to enter this world in July so we wished to ensure that our legal status was correct and anyway we felt that it was time to get married. Mandy and I had

186

begun to live together 'officially' around August 1984 when
I moved from Blessington to Sherlockstown. We didn't make
a conscious, momentous, agonising decision about it — we
just went ahead and did it: it seemed the perfectly natural
thing to do.

We did however have one specific shared principle about
our future life together. We resolved not to have a serious
row or let any disagreement develop into a verbal marathon,
or a spiteful short sprint, or indulge in saying something
that we could regret later, just for the sake of scoring points.

In the seven years that we have been together we have
observed this agreement fully. We have had our own little
disagreements but we have sorted them out calmly. It takes
a lot of willpower and restraint at times but if you have mutual
love and respect as the central core of your relationship it
becomes routine to button up the lips and shift one's
thoughts to something else. Thank God it works for us — it
takes patience, but, believe me, it is worth the effort. I
suppose a very pertinent reason for our compatibility is that
we don't compete with each other or feel any need to do so.
Lynne often claims, totally without foundation of course, that
I can maintain the peace with Mandy because I can go into
the office every morning and eat the head off her (Lynne).
What a joke! There may be a scintilla of a grain of truth
there occasionally but on a regular basis — never!

As I've told you, when I met Mandy in July 1984 I was
good and ready for her. She was my oasis after so many
mirages. She allowed me to park my weary spirit beside her
and offered me the haven of her body and soul. At last, life
began to make sense and I had a beautifully serene,
thoughtful partner to share it with me.

For a long time after we met I still felt angry and hurt
over the previous few years. This fury was directed at no-one
in particular and I wasn't blaming anybody except myself. I
had developed an instinctive distrust of women and of my

relationships with them. I found it difficult to relate to them because of my confused feelings — me, Mick Doyle who can rationalise most things in life and make sense of them — couldn't put two sentences together talking to a girl.

I couldn't trust myself to relax in case I got hurt again. I almost needed a guarantee in writing that nobody would take advantage of my feelings. Sex, funnily enough, had nothing to do with it. I could have sex anytime I wanted, and did. But I craved for more than just sex: body and soul, I wanted a girl whom I could love and who would love me in return. As Neil Diamond says in his song *I am, I said*: . . .

'But I've got an emptiness deep inside,
And I tried but it won't let me go,
Now I'm not a man who likes to swear
But I've never cared for the sound of being alone.'

Whatever about the swearing I can identify with those feelings exactly. I was lucky, however, that I didn't succumb to self-pity and self-hate because these are twin pathological terrors which can destroy you. I am basically a positive person and I could luckily identify these negative emotions in their embryonic stages, pick them up, look them straight in the eye and dump them. Three things kept me going. I was busy at work, coaching Leinster was a labour of love and I jogged a lot. I jogged a good five miles early every morning — the best therapy in the world. The pheromones released by such physical, aerobic activity calmed the neurotic centres and helped me to maintain an equilibrium.

Mind you there were also nights of extreme loneliness when I drank myself into oblivion, by myself, trying to forget the hurt and not really wanting to face the future.

I went through my own pain barrier in the summer of 1984 and emerged from it whole and entire about two weeks after meeting Mandy. There is no doubt that my time of crisis did me a lot of good in the longer term and, I hope, made me a better person. I certainly developed a much

nore balanced understanding of men's relationships with
vomen. I recognised and analysed the areas where I had
allen down before in my relationships, particularly with
_ynne and to a lesser extent with Maria. I saw my own faults
ind shortcomings more clearly. I know that I became a
nuch more rounded, better person and I even found myself
:asier to live with. Then came Mandy, the catalyst for my
1ew life. Without her I would still be floundering. For a young
voman she possessed a profound insight into life and love.

For Christmas 1984 I bought Mandy a ring. Now, it wasn't
neant to be an engagement ring — just a ring, possibly a
cind of engagement kind of a ring or maybe an eternity
ing. Anyway, it was a nice ring and it doubled as an engage-
nent ring when it was needed. It was a 'whatever you're
1aving yourself' kind of a ring.

We assumed we were engaged anyway so there was no big
leal about it and we were having a romantic life together.
Marriage had not surfaced at this time and we were both
>pen-minded about it. Since I was not yet divorced there
vas no practical question of getting married.

Quite candidly I was apprehensive on two counts. First, I
vas dreadfully afraid that our beautiful, loving relationship
vould change if we got married and that the dreaded scourge
>f role-playing would emerge; and secondly, I was unsure if
 could face again the natural expression of married love —
>abies.

Lynne and I were divorced in Bristol in 1987 and I was
ree to contract a marriage with the spinster Power-Smith if
ve both wished it. It was Emma's impending arrival that
nade our minds up and I wrote a little note to Mandy one
1ight over dinner asking her to marry me. It reads as follows:

'Amanda P-S, will you make a happily married man *again*
>ut of me?

Yours forever, and always as well,

Gobnait.'

We decided to have a very small, intimate, quiet wedding in Omagh. Hugh Gibson and George (Baggy) James were to be my second best men. I insisted on being best man myself and one look at Mandy's obvious state of impending motherhood proved my point exactly. Sharon and Amanda, my daughters, 'gave me away'. My cousin Marie Dennehy ensured that I did everything right. All Mandy's family attended and ate all the food: my side did all the drinking. Our friends Ronnie and Lyla Steel added to the enjoyment of the day and kept the numbers right on my side! So did Bob and Alice Brady.

The day was crisp and clear and Amy McAleer's wedding ceremony was beautiful, simple and absolutely perfect. The *Sunday Independent* and *Sunday Press* had sent up two photographers and we accommodated them for their interest and their efforts by having the photographs before the wedding ceremony. One particular shot of Mandy in my arms, which made the papers, only showed us from the waist up, which was just as well because my feet were sinking into the soft mud at the end of the lawn. Omagh Registry Office is a beautiful redbrick building in lovely surroundings. The place exudes charm and taste and I was proud, delighted and happy that my Mandy and I were married there.

The atrocities took place afterwards in the Killyhevlin Hotel in Enniskillen and we had an eventful day. We shared a huge square of tables so that everybody could see and speak to everyone else. Most people made unscheduled speeches or sang and we had a happy memorable wedding. Emma now intimates that she enjoyed it herself.

Poor Mandy had had serious morning sickness for every day of her pregnancy and she was one happy lady on the 17 July 1989 at 5.30 p.m. in Clane Maternity Hospital when she gave birth to a bouncing Emma Louise Doyle. In fact we both gave birth to her! I did so much deep breathing and pushing by myself in the process that the doctor almost expected me to produce something myself. Emma is now a beautiful little madam and my three eldest love playing with their little sister. It is quite different having a baby now and watching her develop than it was when Lynne and I started our family. For a start I 'assisted' at the birth. Also, Emma has never been in a cot — she shared our bed since the day she was born and we have had no sleepless nights. I haven't had anyway!

Mandy breastfed her or more correctly Emma helped herself at any time during the night she wished and many times during the day. Mandy's mothering instincts and the logical ways she has with Emma are inspiring to say the least. I always thought Dr Spock was a bit of a know-all and a pain in the arse to boot. Now I *know* that he was. The professional advice and literature on motherhood and child rearing available nowadays is excellent and a far cry from the 'medicine man' theories of yesteryear.

One truly amazing feature about Emma's behaviour is, to me at any rate, that she doesn't suck her thumb or put things in her mouth. No doubt the fact that she had Mandy's milk on a self-service basis generated confidence in her and prompted the thought that the 'oral' phase in a baby's development is a reflection of insecurity and the loss of the mother's breast rather than a genuine childish curiosity. Intriguing little beings, babies! I'm looking forward to a little brother for her. I must tell Mandy one of these days.

I almost forgot the honeymoon! We spent an idyllic week at Rathsallagh, Dunlavin Co. Wicklow, the home of Kay and Joe O'Flynn. I wrote my weekly article for the *Evening Herald* from there which began as follows:

'This epistle, dear reader, is coming to you from paradise; a perfumed garden called Rathsallagh, down in County Wicklow where the resident, ministering angels, Kay and Joe O'Flynn, are nurturing myself and the comely Amanda in a cocoon of self-indulgent escapism. Here, half way between Dunlavin and Grangecon, everything is at peace

with nature's ways. The ewes are about to lamb and are so
laid back about the impending event that not even shouting
'mint sauce and lamb chops' at them would worry a furrow
on to their sheeply brows.

'Rathsallagh, far, far from the madding crowd, would
blush at the mention of Salman Rushdie, Edwina Currie or
the old reliable *Salmonesbec enteritidis.*

'Here the pheasants strut about the estate in mimicry of
the jack-booted sentinels of the Third Reich. They are so
bloody arrogant that, should you disrupt their daily walkabout you are liable to receive the "two feather" gesture that
is the avian version of a Harvey Smith!'

Rathsallagh was and is a heavenly spot and my scribbling
could not do it full justice.

But there is always sadness and reality in the midst of
such happiness. We attended the funeral of my friend
Brendan McGuckian, a lovely, lovable gentleman, who had
died tragically in a freak accident on Sunday 12 March. It
was heartbreaking to see the dignity and bewildered hurt in
his beautiful wife Frances' face and his dear children. I felt
guilty for being happy and thankful for being alive. Brendan
was a man who touched a chord in everyone who came in
contact with him and personally I miss him and am grateful
that I knew him. I hope Frances and the children have found
their peace and that they will know love and happiness again.
They at least have beautiful memories of an exceptional
lovely man.

I am a very lucky man and I am grateful for it. I feel
privileged to have come from the family, the county and the
background that I do. I have been fortunate in coming into
contact with all the people I have met during my first fifty
years on this earth. I am thankful for the opportunities with
which I was presented and proud of those that I took up.

My profession, veterinary, and my sport, rugby, have been
decisive influences in my life and both have taught me that

problems are merely opportunities travelling incognito; they have made me considerate in success and philosophical in failure; they have taught me that failure is only success delayed. Rugby and my profession have brought balance, depth and perspective to my life; they have taught me that honesty has no substitute; they have given me the confidence to recognise what is happening around me, to assess it realistically and the self-belief to make positive decisions.

I am intolerant of vacillation, equivocation and waffle; I do not care much for people who rush to judge others. I am wary of those who continually promote their reasoned objectivity but are cunningly camouflaging their actions — but not well enough. As Bob Dylan said, 'Sometimes Satan comes as a man of peace.' I am indebted to all those who have trusted me and for giving me responsibility and opportunity. I thank all the players, selectors and administrations who believed in me and who took up the challenges like men.

Rugby is an honest game: I hope it remains that way. The ethos is more important than the status. Rugby has taught me humility and pride — but I suppose being a Kerryman pride has been with me always. Rugby has set me challenges that have helped to shape and develop me. It has given me an insight into human nature and generated in me a huge respect for the unlimited scope and flexibility of the mind and spirit. I measure success differently to most scribes. For me it lies mostly in the performance and the pursuit of excellence.

Results are the province of statisticians. The mentality of playing 'not to lose' has no place in my lexicon. It is an insult to the human spirit not to reach out for the ultimate and use all your talents — win, lose or draw.

Reflecting on my life I suppose I am at times bemused by it all. I am glad I stood up to be counted and I am proud of what I have done. If I have any regret it is that I have taken fifty years to grow up! I am immensely proud of my extended family and heartily thankful for the two women — Lynne and Mandy — who have given me so much. I am happy that Lynne and I faced up to our personal problems with love, dignity, respect and courage and that we helped each other and our children through very traumatic times. I am grateful to the friends and family who supported us and gave us correct advice and much understanding.

I am hugely indebted to Dr Sharp and the staff of the Coronary Unit in Auckland General Hospital, without whom I possibly would not be here now and to the Man above for sparing me.

Writing one's autobiography at the half-way stage in one's life — the magical fifty years — is, I suppose, a bit daft! Being fifty years old, which I was on 13 October 1990, is like a 'safe period'. Tom Clifford, who died recently, a legend in Irish and Lions rugby, once described a safe period as half-time against Young Munster.

Writing this book has generated many emotions in me — some sad, some wistful, the vast majority of extreme happiness. Certainly, there are no regrets and no anger.

There are many things yet that I want to do with my life and leisure. I just hope that the next fifty years are half as good as the last.

I have enjoyed writing this book even if nobody reads it! When I started out to write this story of my life Rosemary McHale, Andrew's godmother, and Sean's cultured other half, advised me: 'Mick, look back at the past, but don't stare.' Not bad advice but I'm afraid I have stared at much of my past and enjoyed it funnily enough.

It has already profited me by reminding me of who I am, where I came from and to whom I am beholden. It has given me a new lease of life and opened up a new exciting vista. Mandy is the love of my life and it would not have much purpose for me without her.

So there you have it. That's my story. I suppose you think you know it all now warts and all. You do in your arse: you don't even know the half of it!